Gold, Silk, Pioneers & Mail

The Story of the Pacific Mail Steamship Company

PACIFIC HISTORY SERIES

Number 6

Other books in the Pacific Maritime History Series:

1. *Beyond the Lagoon*, by Lyndall Landauer.
2. *The Voyages of the Ship* Revere, *1849-1883* by M. R. Gleason.
3. *Clipper Ship Captain, Daniel McLaughlin and the* Glory of the Seas, by Michael J. Mjelde.
4 *The White Flyers,* Harvard *and* Yale, *American Coastwise Travel*, by George F. Gruner.
5. *Steel Ships and Iron Pipe, Western Pipe and Steel Company of California, the Company, the Yard, the Ships*, by Dean L. Mawdsley.

Gold, Silk, Pioneers & Mail

The Story of the Pacific Mail Steamship Company

BY

ROBERT J. CHANDLER, Ph.D.
STEPHEN J. POTASH

Foreword by

James P. Delgado, Ph.D.

Friends of the San Francisco Maritime Museum Library

San Francisco

2007

Cover:
Lithograph of the steamer *China* (I) by Endicott & Co. of New York, ca. 1867, from the Collection of Stephen J. and Jeremy W. Potash. Photograph by Cathy Forbes.

Portions of this work originally appeared in *The Argonaut,* Vol. 16, No. 1, Summer 2005, San Francisco Museum and Historical Society.

The Glencannon Press, Palo Alto, California.
Printed in the United States of America
Second Printing, 2009
Published by: Friends of the National Maritime Museum Library at San Francisco Maritime
                       National Historical Park.

ISBN-13: 978-1-889901-41-1
ISBN-10: 1-889901-41-5
LCCN 2007926164

COPYRIGHT 2007 BY STEPHEN J. POTASH AND ROBERT J. CHANDLER

DEDICATED TO

W.B. (Bruce) Seaton

Chairman of American President Lines from 1977-1992,
who recognized that the past is glorious
when it helps to define a clear vision of the future,

and

John Haskell Kemble

Professor of History at Pomona College,
Claremont, California, from 1936 to 1977,
whose brilliant research revealed that glorious past.

ILLUSTRATIONS

S.S. *Tennessee*, lithograph, ca. 1849 — 2

Brass bag tag, c. 1860 — 2

Letter cover, Steamer *California*, 1849 — 3

S.S. *Golden Gate*, lithograph, 1862 — 4

Song sheet, 1862 — 5

San Francisco in 1849, lithograph, ca. 1849 — 6

S.S. *Uncle Sam*, lithograph, ca. 1852 — 7

S.S. *Golden City*, photograph ca. 1865 — 7

S.S. *San Francisco*, lithograph, 1854 — 9

Opposition Line Steerage ticket, ca.1866 — 12

S.S. *John L. Stephens*, lithograph, ca. 1852 — 13

S.S. *Colorado*, lithograph, 1865 — 14

S.S. *Constitution*, lithograph, ca. 1861 — 16

Only a Headache, ca. 1865 — 17

Letter cover, Steamer *Sacramento*, 1865 — 19

1855 letter "Too Late" — 20

Advertisement, 1869 — 22

Wells Fargo Receipt, S.S. *Orizaba*, 1864 — 23

Loading S.S. *Arizona* at Aspinwall, ca. 1865 — 25

Pacific Mail Silver Tureen, presented 1853 — 26

Presentation Goblet, S.S. *Sacramento*, 1869 — 28

S.S. *China* (I), lithograph, ca. 1867 — 32

S.S. *China* (II), post card, ca. 1889 — 33

S.S. *Japan*, stereopticon, ca. 1870 — 34

Steerage aboard S.S. *Alaska*, lithograph, 1876 — 35

S.S. *Great Republic*, lithograph, ca. 1867 — 36

S.S. *China*, *America* meet mid-Pacific, 1870 — 37

S.S. *City of Rio de Janeiro*, stereopticon, 1898 — 37

S.S. *City of Peking*, oil painting, ca. 1874 — 38

S.S. *City of Peking* at War, lithograph, 1898 — 38

S.S. *Korea*, lithograph, 1903 — 39

S.S. *Manchuria*, oil painting, ca. 1904 — 39

S.S. *City of Sydney*, oil painting, ca. 1875 — 40

S.S. *Stanley Dollar*, oil painting, 1902 — 40

S.S. *President Wilson*, menu, 1934 — 41

S.S. *President Lincoln*, literature, 1924 — 41

S.S. *President Hoover*, poster, 1938 — 43

PMSS complex, Benicia, lithograph ca. 1879 — 44

PMSS coaling office, photo, 2007 — 44

PMSS foundry, photo, 2007 — 44

The printer's device above and at the start of each section is the monogram "PMSSCo"
from a deck of Pacific Mail playing cards in the Potash collection.

ACKNOWLEDGEMENTS

Several people merit special BOOMS from the signal cannon for their role in bringing this project to fruition. James P. Delgado, a former Maritime Historian for the National Park Service in San Francisco who now serves as Executive Director of the Institute of Nautical Archeology based in College Station, Texas, contributed the Foreword. Dr. Delgado is the recognized authority today on West Coast maritime history. His personal archaelogical investigations of several Pacific Mail vessels add excitement and realism to the story, and his broad perspective on the company's place in history truly enhances the value of this small tome. Special thanks go to Charles Fracchia, founding President and President-for-Life, regardless of his title, of the San Francisco Museum and Historical Society, who invited us to create the article on Pacific Mail for the Society's journal, The Argonaut, that eventually became the core of this book. We deeply appreciate the guidance, support and careful copy-editing of David Hull, Principal Librarian of the San Francisco Maritime National Historical Park, and the Publication Committee of the Friends of the San Francisco Maritime Museum Library, which accepted this book for publication as the latest in their Pacific Maritime History Series. Thanks also to Cathy Forbes and the Benicia Historical Society for their generous support of our efforts, and for their ongoing enthusiasm to preserve the sole remaining Pacific Mail facilities, the coaling office and the foundry in Benicia, California. Cathy Forbes and Richard Langs produced the quality photography for this publication. And, finally, we offer a loving salute to our Commodores, Susan L. Chandler and Jeremy W. Potash, who tolerate — nay, even encourage — the passion we share for California's colorful maritime history.

R.J.C.
S.J.P

CONTENTS

FOREWORD.. ix

1   PIONEERING U.S. FLAG STEAMSHIP COMPANY............................ 1

2   INVESTING IN THE FUTURE... 3

3   RUNNING A STEAMSHIP IS NOT CHEAP.. 8

4   PAY TO RIDE.. 10

5   THE MAIL MUST GO THROUGH!.. 15

6   STAGECOACHES BRING COMPETITION: THE OVERLAND MAIL.............. 21

7   WELLS FARGO & CO.'S EXPRESS LEADS...................................... 24

8   SAILING ALONG WITH PACIFIC MAIL.. 28

9   TO CHINA AND BEYOND.. 33

EPILOGUE.. 44

END NOTES.. 45

BIBLIOGRAPHY.. 46

ABOUT THE AUTHORS.. 49

INDEX.. 50

FOREWORD

One of the first acts of the newly independent United States was the dispatch, by a group of merchants, of a ship into the Pacific to trade directly with China. The China Trade dominated America's maritime mercantile endeavors. It inspired other markets, such as California's hide and tallow trade, the South Pacific's trade in sandalwood and beche de mer, and the maritime fur trade on the Northwest Coast of America.

American desires to dominate the China Trade, and by extension, the entire Pacific Basin and all of its trade, focused on establishing a base — an entrepot, or a zone of free exchange — on the western shores of the American continent. From such a port, American ships could fill the ocean, fed by regular supply from the East Coast. That port was San Francisco, settled by Spain in the last quarter of the eighteenth century and under Mexican control by the second quarter of the nineteenth century. American plans for the acquisition of California began with an offer to purchase in 1835 and ended in conquest as an act of war in 1846. The discovery of gold in California in 1848 and the resultant rush propelled San Francisco's rapid rise as a city and as America's principal port on the Pacific.

The way of the future was clear. A new empire was rising that would soon encompass the Pacific and the Far East. In 1855, San Francisco's first historians commented:

> Not only are Japan and China much nearer to the California coast than India is to England; but with the aid of steam the time for accomplishing the distance is immensely reduced ... So it was with the English in India; and so it may be with the Americans in China. Just give us *time*. England has not been very scrupulous in her stealthy progress over Hindostan, Ceylon and Birmah. Then neither need America fear her reproaches, if she, in like manner, conquer, or annex the Sandwich Islands, the Islands of Japan, those of the great Malayan Archipelago, or the mighty "Flowery Empire" itself. A few more years, and a few millions of Americans in the Pacific may realize the gigantic scheme ... The railway across, or *through* the Snowy and Rocky Mountains, which will bind all North America with its iron arm into one mighty empire, will facilitate the operation. And then SAN FRANCISCO — in the execution and triumph of that scheme, will assuredly become what Liverpool, or even London is to England, and what New York is to the Middle and Eastern states of America — a grand depot for numerous manufactures and produce, and a harbor for the fleets of every nation." (Soulé *et al.* *Annals of San Francisco.* 1855:54-55)

The tools of the new empire were determination, capital, and technology. Technology arrived not only on rails of iron stretching across the continent in 1869, but in ships of wood, propelled by steam, that opened the North Pacific Coast during the Gold Rush years of 1848-1851. These pioneer steamships gave way to larger vessels that began regular service across the Pacific to China and Japan in 1867, opening the way for an American Empire in the Pacific.

Most of these ships belonged to one commercial enterprise, the Pacific Mail Steamship Company of New York. Chartered by an Act of Congress, financed with government subsidy and backed by shipping merchants with long experience in the China Trade, the PMSSC was the pioneer steamship line of the American

Pacific. Connecting via the narrow isthmus of Panama to steamers from New York and New Orleans, the Pacific Mail's steamers ran along the *Coast Pilot*'s Seventh Sheet Frontside Chart north from Panama City, to San Francisco and then to Portland, Oregon.

The fortuitous accident of the California Gold Rush made the fortunes of the Pacific Mail and its backers. The fleet, beginning with three small wooden steamers, expanded with the demand for passage to California. The Pacific Mail's steamships carried not only passengers but also mail, high value freight, and gold. The PMSSC was the connective link of empire between the coasts. It spurred the construction of a railroad across Panama, and renewed discussion of a canal to cut through the same route. Competitors — other steamship lines, other routes via Mexico and Nicaragua — appeared, but never seriously challenged the Pacific Mail. The Company thrived despite competition, shipwrecks, and the Civil War. The Pacific Mail built the first major industrial facility on the Pacific Coast when it opened a marine depot and engine foundry at Benicia, on San Francisco Bay, in 1851, and added to its fleet, building larger, more powerful steamers to ply the coast.

The extension of the Pacific Mail's mandate to transpacific trade, again by Act of Congress, added new vessels to the fleet and a new role. The riches of the Far East, packed into the holds of the steamers, began to arrive in San Francisco, as did increasing numbers of Asian (largely Chinese) immigrants. San Francisco boomed again as a port. Now America's gateway to Asia and Asia's gateway into America, the city, its surrounding region, and the nation were enriched and forever changed by the voyages of the steamers of the Pacific Mail Steamship Company.

For such a significant history, there is amazingly little left to represent the Company's achievements. The Company offices are long gone, victims of fire and urban renewal, the corporate archives for the most part destroyed by fire save those preserved in the holdings of the Henry E. Huntington Library

in Pasadena, and to a lesser extent, at the Bancroft Library in Berkeley. The depot at Benicia closed in the last century, but some of its brick buildings still stand on the shores of Carquinez Strait. On the shores of Belvedere, the social saloon of the P.M.S.S. *China* (I), one of the Company's four steamers built in 1866 to inaugurate the transpacific trade, stands as a museum operated by the Belvedere Tiburon Landmarks Society. Small and exquisite, the "*China* Cabin" speaks to the elegance of these vanished leviathans of the Pacific.

As an archaeologist, I have encountered other relics of the Pacific Mail: the broken remnants of the Pacific Mail steamer *Tennessee*, wrecked in her namesake cove on Marin County's coast in March 1853; the sunken remains of the steamer *Winfield Scott*, wrecked off Southern California's Anacapa Island in December 1853; and the recently identified remains of the transpacific steamer *Great Republic*, contemporary of *China*, which wrecked at the mouth of the Columbia River in April 1879. These diving adventures were matched by another encounter at Candlestick Cove, where sewer construction in 1989 hit a buried iron hulk on the landfilled shore. I was called in to identify the hulk — only the bottom of a scrapped out vessel of some considerable size — and was able to identify it as the remains of the P.M.S.S. *City of Peking*, hauled into Candlestick Cove to be scrapped at the end of her long career. Cut down to below the waterline, the lower hull, massive frames and sheared-off rivets of the steamer still rest, unmarked and again forgotten, as thousands of cars race past on Highway 101.

There have been histories written, notably by John Haskell Kemble, Dean of Pacific Coast maritime historians. Kemble's pioneering articles on the Pacific Mail, and his landmark work, *The Panama Route*, all published in the 1940s, remain standard and invaluable resources. Ernest Wiltsee's epic book on Gold Rush steamships is another, as is John Niven's 1987 book on the American President Lines and its predecessors (notably the PMSSC) The Book Club of California produced, under Kemble's editorship, a series of keepsakes on Gold Rush steamers, including a number of the Pacific Mail's most famous ships.

However, for all these magnificent publications, there has not been, until now, a focused, in-depth look at the Pacific Mail Steamship Company for more than fifty years. Robert J. Chandler and Steve Potash have now done so in this magnificent new monograph. Using one of the richest bibliographies ever compiled on the company, they have integrated material about the Pacific Mail's operations, management and fleets through the merger into the Dollar Line in 1927 and the transition to American President Lines in 1938, to the current ownership of the formerly U.S.-flagged company by an agency of the Government of Singapore.

They have also drawn on the diverse and significant personal collection each author holds — Chandler's incredible Pacific Mail collection of ephemera and Potash's unique collection of Pacific Mail art, lithographs, silver and other artifacts, including a rare survival, a fragile "throw-away" tea caddy from the Company's China Trade. A number of their items are like this — originals or one of a kind, which have never before been published. They have included in their captions interesting and colorful anecdotes about the personalities associated with the Company, its art, and its ships. This rich illustrated record also, as never before, provides a sweeping documentary of the steamers from 1849 through to the modern liner era.

The core of the Pacific Mail's business was carrying people, gold and the mail. In areas such as express and letter delivery, Chandler and Potash have more fully delineated these important aspects of shipping and its impact on the social and business life of California than anyone has before. Drawing on a rich trove of unpublished manuscript letters and diaries, they also evoke life aboard the Pacific Mail steamers. Readers of this monograph will leave with a firsthand understanding of the shipboard experience of the Pacific Mail's passengers in the pioneer days of the Gold Rush and the first voyages by steam to the Far East. This concise, wonderfully illustrated, inexpensive monograph is a wonderful and welcome addition, and I know that Jack Kemble would be pleased and proud. My only wish is that Jack could have written this foreword.

James P. Delgado
Maritime Archaeologist, Historian, and Author of *To California By Sea: A Maritime History of the Gold Rush.* (University of South Carolina Press, 1990)

PIONEERING U.S. FLAG STEAMSHIP COMPANY

In 1847, William Henry Aspinwall had a dream with a specific Pacific vision. This merchant, whose sail-driven packet ships traded with Europe, South America, and China, would start a steamship line to deliver mail and passengers along the west coast of North America.

What spurred this dream? In 1846, as wagon trains rolled in to settle Oregon, the United States snagged California as booty during the Mexican War. On November 19, 1847, Aspinwall acquired the government mail contract; on January 4, 1848, shipyard workers laid the keel for the first of his three sidewheel steamships; on April 12, he incorporated the Pacific Mail Steamship Company; and on October 6, his first steamer departed for California service.

The arrival and departure of the Pacific Mail steamers became a cycle of life for Californians. These four days a month provided the only contact with the outside world. When the semaphore on Telegraph Hill showed both arms horizontal, San Franciscans expected a sidewheel steamer. Soon the "BOOOOMMMM" of her cannon reverberating across the city told all of her arrival. A rush to the dock, post, and express offices followed. All sought letters.

Steamer Day, the frantic day before the steamer sailed, became an institution. "The people of California and San Francisco seem to count time," the San Francisco *Alta California* remarked in 1854, "from Steamer Day to Steamer Day." In January 1857, one San Franciscan did not look upon it so fondly. "A proper bad day is that ill, dismal-sounding 'Steamer Day,'" he complained. Money made him mad, he explained: Steamer Day is "'pay up' day," and therefore "a day *dreaded* by most Californians." Ritually, merchants settled accounts, friends said good-bye, and all wrote letters.[1]

The rush of humanity westward to California meant money was to be made. Service on the Atlantic Ocean from New York City to Aspinwall, known as Colón today, remained unsatisfactory. Poor food, cramped conditions, rolling ships, bad seamanship, and maritime disasters so characterized the United States Mail Line that with the end of its mail contract in 1859, it went out of business. The Pacific Mail assumed control of that route as well on November 1, 1865.

Just as blood upon the water attracts sharks, paying passengers drew rivals in the steamship business. Through 1854, a host of competitors surfaced on both oceans, but soon it came down to one — Cornelius Vanderbilt. The "Commodore," a natural and gifted businessman, was vicious, ruthless, and a penny-pincher. From 1848 through 1865, he fought the Pacific Mail on both oceans, with a few periods of cooperation. Travel conditions on his ships remained deplorable for fifteen years.

In contrast, those who ran the Pacific Mail cultivated a sense of honesty and service. Atlantic conditions improved only after November 1, 1865, when the Pacific Mail took control. Good service was expensive, and passengers paid a higher amount for it.

SS **TENNESSEE** – *Some say you can still see the tired bones and occasional engine parts of the Steamer* **Tennessee**
*during low tide at Tennessee Cove in Marin County where she went down, just four miles north of the entrance to
San Francisco Bay. Launched in 1848 and acquired by Pacific Mail the following year, this wooden side-wheeler brought
miners to the San Francisco Gold Rush and relayed them, their treasures, and the mails back to Panama,
from whence they made their way back up the east coast. She broke up against the Marin rocks in 1853.
This ca. 1849 lithograph by Sarony & Major of New York bears a brass plate indicating it was owned by
Renee Pierre Schwerin, a 19th Century Vice President and the General Manager of Pacific Mail, who ran the company
from San Francisco when it came under the control of railroad tycoon Collis P. Huntington.
From the collection of Stephen J. and Jeremy W. Potash. Photo by Cathy Forbes.*

Beginning in 1869, immigrants could reach California by railroad in less than a third of the time required to travel by ship. Then memories of the Panama route with its wooden paddlers faded. In turn, the Pacific Mail steamed toward the setting sun. Once again, it pioneered a new route, creating the first regularly-scheduled trans-Pacific steamship trade. Later, its modern-day successors brought container shipping to new heights through technological innovation. Today the venerable American carrier that in 1849 sailed the first steamer into San Francisco Bay is steered from Singapore.

*Passengers checked up to 100 pounds of luggage free and received two brass tags. One went with the luggage,
while the owner kept the duplicate. Come join intrepid traveler #927 in Cabin D, "2nd Cabin" on a voyage of adventure.
Collection of Robert J. Chandler.*

INVESTING IN THE FUTURE

In late 1847, Aspinwall ordered three 1,100-ton wooden steamers. The *California, Panama,* and *Oregon* were all about 220 feet in length, with 34-foot beams, and accommodations for seventy-five passengers from first class to steerage. William H. Webb built the *California* and the *Panama,* while the neighboring yard of Stephen Smith and John Dimon built the *Oregon.* These were the first ocean-going American steamships to have diagonal cross-beam iron strapping reinforcing their long hulls.

Webb was a remarkable shipbuilder and a founding director of the Pacific Mail. He took over his father Isaac's yard in 1840, built the finest clipper ships, and then turned to steam navigation. In all, Webb launched 135 wooden ships, and

On July 30, 1849, the prominent mercantile firm of [Henry] Mellus, [William Davis Merry] Howard & Co. wrote a commercial letter to Boston marked to be sent collect by the pioneer steamer California. The steamer sailed August 2, and reached Panama on August 24. September 15, a month and a half after departure, found the letter in Boston. From the collection of Robert Chandler.

in 1894, he opened the Webb Institute of Naval Architecture.

The *California,* which builder Webb found to be "a good sea boat," expected difficulties. She sailed for San Francisco in October 1848 with a duplicate set of engine parts, because there were no repair facilities in the isolated land. As the steamer rounded South America, President James K. Polk told Congress on December 5, that California was filled with gold. The Gold Rush was on! When she stopped at Panama in late January, a mob awaited her, and on February 28, 1849, the appropriately named *California* sailed into San Francisco carrying 365 Argonauts, plus her crew of 34.[2]

Thomas Rainey, who in 1858 published a study of steamship costs, declared that the Pacific Mail had "the finest steam fleet in the United States." It contracted with New York shipbuilders to develop large, fast, comfortable ships for the Pacific. Their designs influenced liners on the Atlantic. Of course as newer ships came along, older ones went into the reserve fleet or were sold to run coastwise between San Diego and Victoria, British Columbia.[3]

The Pacific Mail ran forty-seven steamers in the first twenty years. In the 1850s, four ships made the most trips, carried the most passengers, and represented that generation of paddlers. They were the *Golden Age, Golden Gate, John L. Stephens,* and *Sonora.* Steerage passengers holed up in the fore part of the ship and hold, while first and second class passengers luxuriated on long, shaded decks, and in cabins center and aft. Both classes ate in

SS **GOLDEN GATE** – *Currier &
Ives were in the business of reporting
the news using lithographed
illustrations, and surviving copies
became rare because they were
tossed out like "yesterday's old
newspaper." In 1862, this
hand-colored print and its caption
reported the tragic loss of Pacific
Mail's SS* **Golden Gate** *off
the coast of Mexico, along with
$1,400,000 in gold treasure and
a huge loss of lives. The vessel was
en route from San Francisco to
Panama. From the collection of
Stephen J. and Jeremy W. Potash.
Photo by Cathy Forbes.*

the same dining room and from the same menu,
but first class grabbed the choicest times.

In 1851, William H. Webb built the *Golden
Gate* with a new design, one to accommodate a
large number of passengers. She was 2,100 tons,
270 feet long, 40 feet wide, and carried 800
passengers — 300 in cabins, 500 in steerage. Two
oscillating engines of British design provided
1,150 horsepower to drive 32-foot diameter paddle
wheels. In case the Navy wanted to saw off the top
deck for conversion into a warship, the engines sat
below the waterline. In 1852, the *Golden Gate* set a
record of 290 miles in a day, steaming at 12 knots,
but using sixty tons of coal. In April 1853, this
"steam clipper" arrived in San Francisco in eleven
days, fourteen hours. Excluding time spent in
Acapulco coaling, she steamed along at 12.6 knots
during her ten days, twenty hours at sea. She was,
as Webb wrote, "a fast and excellent sea boat."[4]

Not all shared Webb's opinion of his ship.
On March 2, 1858, former passenger William
H. Howland wrote his father to say "We have got
to California safe." He added, "I believe for the
pleasure of the journey, I would rather cross the
plains." He made these remarks after a record-
setting trip from the east.

"We was only 8 days from New York [on the
Moses Taylor] to our first landing place the Isthmus,"
he wrote, "and met with good luck to take the
[railroad] cars in three hours or a little more, and
in about four hours we got across the Isthmus to
Panama, where we got rite on the boat [*Golden
Gate*] and sailed rite through without delays. We
got to San Francisco the 26th." The 500 passengers
made this fast trip, the *Alta* reported, "in 21 days, 22
1/2 hours, from wharf to wharf, being the shortest
passage made from New York."[5]

The worst fear at sea became the "fire fiend."
For the fast *Golden Gate*, this evil would eventually
devour her. In addition to being built of wood,
these ships burst with combustibles. Coal was
provided for fuel. Hay was carried as fresh food
for livestock. Both could combust spontaneously.
At least once during a voyage, the captain's shrill
whistle sent the crew to fire stations, with hoses
spewing water, and the life boats immediately
swung out. However, such precautions saved
neither the *Golden Gate* in 1862, the *America* in
1872, nor the *Japan* in 1874.

On June 27, 1862, the *Golden Gate* caught fire
off the Mexican coast, killing 175 passengers. It was
the only loss of life on a Pacific Mail steamer prior
to completion of the transcontinental railroad in
1869. Salvors through the years recovered most of
the treasure. Her bell rings in the rare book section
of San Francisco's Main Public Library.

Stephen Smith and John Dimon constructed
the reliable two-stacker *John L. Stephens*, named for a
Pacific Mail and Panama Railroad director following
his death from malaria. She was slightly larger than
the *Golden Gate*, at 274 feet in length, 43 feet in
beam, with 32-foot diameter wheels, and powered

by a similar 640-horsepower engine. Bunkers held 450 tons of coal. After her years with the Pacific Mail, the *John L. Stephens* saw service until 1878.

The 1853 *Golden Age*, at 2,300 tons, was the largest yet. She measured 273 feet, with a 42-foot beam, and accommodated 1,200 passengers – 200 first cabin, 200 second cabin, and 800 steerage. She sailed as the final ship William H. Brown built and became his masterpiece. Her first sailings were long, to and from Australia, and a 1,350-horsepower exposed walking-beam engine drove 34-foot diameter wheels. The *Golden Age* carried 1,200 tons of coal and 500 tons of cargo.

She also became the fastest vessel in the Pacific Mail fleet. In 1858, she set a record from Panama of 11 days, 7.5 hours. Deducting eight hours spent at Acapulco and Manzanillo, the *Golden Age* sped along at 12.3 knots. While her speed was a mite slower that the *Golden Gate* in 1853, she spent less time in way ports. Finally scrapped in 1890, she was one of the earliest Gold Rush paddlers built, and the last left.

In 1854, Jacob A. Westervelt & Co. built the fourth of the old regulars, the 269 by 36-foot *Sonora*. She and her Atlantic sistership *St. Louis* were the only vessels in the fleet built in the

"I Don't Want to be Drowned" lamented passengers aboard the stricken **Golden Gate** *after the pride of the Pacific Mail's fleet caught fire off the Mexican coast on July 27, 1862. Captain William H. Hudson quickly beached the ship, but the tragedy claimed 175 lives.*
Image from the collection of Robert Chandler.

British style with the boilers behind the engines. With coal storage of 550 tons, a 675-horsepower walking-beam engine drove 30-foot paddle wheels. The *Sonora* met her end in spring 1868, broken up on the beach at Sausalito.

Besides ships, the Pacific Mail needed facilities for fuel, passengers, and repair. It quickly established coaling stations at Panama, Acapulco, Benicia, and Astoria, with the main depot at the Mexican port. There the steamer would squeeze between two hulks to be coaled. At great expense, supplies of good European and eastern coal came around Cape Horn.

To land passengers and cargo at San Francisco, in 1850, the Pacific Mail invested in Long Wharf, an extension of Commercial Street, which suited its needs into 1853. The rest of 1853 and 1854 saw the mail steamers arrive at and depart from the Broadway and Pacific Street wharves, until the Pacific Mail settled at the Vallejo Street Wharf. In October 1857, the steamship company moved from Vallejo Street to the deeper water of Folsom Street Wharf below Market Street. In June 1867, the Pacific Mail landed further south at its own wharf at Brannan and First streets.

In May 1850, the Pacific Mail Steamship Company began constructing the first heavy industrial plant on the Pacific coast at Benicia. It maintained a full repair facility and kept back-up steamers. On May 5, 1858, the *Golden Gate*, with $1.9 million in gold aboard, broke her center drive shaft 45 miles beyond the Golden Gate. Limping back on one wheel, she arrived in San Francisco at 6 A.M. the next day. Benicia workmen, who were immediately notified, reassembled the engines of the *Sonora*, then undergoing repair, painted the ship, and within 26 hours had her provisioned, coaled, and ready for sea. The *Sonora* advertised to sail from Folsom Wharf at 5 P.M. on May 7, 1858.[6]

On land as well as sea, President Aspinwall worked to eliminate time from the journey. On April 7, 1849, he formed the Panama Railroad Company. At the cost of 6,000 lives, including what was said to be the death of one laborer per wooden tie laid, the company finished the forty-seven-mile transcontinental railroad on January 28, 1855.

SAN FRANCISCO IN 1849 – As miners poured in by sea and land, the sleepy harbor at San Francisco began to fill with the masts of wooden ships and transition-era steamers from all over the world. Pacific Mail Steamship Company's first San Francisco office can be seen in this detail of a ca. 1849 lithograph "drawn on the spot" by Henry Firks in 1849; it is the three-windowed building located just left of center, and is labeled "PMSS Co" on the exterior wall. The fleet of vessels in the Bay includes two of Pacific Mail's earliest steamers, the SS **Panama** and the SS **Oregon**. From the collection of Stephen J. and Jeremy W. Potash. Photo by Cathy Forbes.

On Valentine's Day 1855, the San Francisco *Herald* rejoiced at this "triumph of American genius and enterprise." The iron horse not only cut transit time from days to hours, but removed the stigma of "unhealthiness" from the Panama route. "Passengers will pass so rapidly through that there will not be time to contract disease," the paper opined.

While the science is a little shaky, the claim to health was important. Disease spread in the confined spaces of a ship. The quotable attorney Oscar L. Shafter had this to say on July 15, 1855: "There were 45 deaths on board the [PMSS] *J.L. Stephens* from the cholera on her passage up [from Panama]. The fact has leaked out this morning and there is a good deal of irritation in the public mind for the reason that none of the papers have noticed the matter. The silence is doubtless the result of an understanding [and probably some money] between the Press and the Steamship Companies."

Route did not matter. On September 15, only two months later, Shafter wrote, "The steamer *Uncle Sam*, belonging to the Nicaragua route, came in yesterday. She had lost 120 of her passengers on her passage by the cholera." He visited the ship's doctor, a "very much exhausted" Russel Fitch, to get the details. Over ten years later, on December 15, 1866, Mark Twain left San Francisco on the *America* by the Nicaragua route, and ran smack into cholera there. The ship arrived back in San Francisco on January 16, 1867, with nine dead.[7]

"Passengers by the *Golden Age* will make the Isthmus Transit BY CARS, over the Panama Railroad, which is now completed from Ocean to Ocean," the Pacific Mail advertised for its steamer sailing on February 16, 1855. The railroad, it claimed, "makes the trip — for Ladies and Children desiring to pass from New York to San Francisco, and vice versa — most comfortable, safe and speedy" and "in less than 6 hours." They paid well for this speed. The Panama Railroad set high rates at $25 per person, included in all steamer fares, and became enormously profitable.[8]

By the early 1860s, steamer architecture and efficiency had improved, and William H. Webb built even larger ships for the Panama route and some even longer to steam to Asia.

SS **UNCLE SAM** – *This handsome paddle-wheeler was built in 1852 for owner-agent Edward Mills, who operated her from Panama to San Francisco in the "Independent Opposition Line" to compete directly with PMSS. Mills sold her in 1854 to Cornelius Vanderbilt. She had various owners and routes, but in 1860 joined Pacific Mail for a time. This Endicott lithograph was made ca. 1852, when Mills owned the ship (EM flag). From the collection of Stephen J. and Jeremy W. Potash. Photo by Cathy Forbes.*

In 1861, Webb blended the best features of the reliable *John L. Stephens* and the *Golden Age* for the *Constitution*. She measured 3,600 tons and stretched 342 by 45 feet. Two boilers, one forward of the engines, one aft, gave her two stacks. With a crew of eighty-five, her economical walking-beam engine drove 40-foot wheels at 10 knots using thirty-nine tons of coal a day, and at 9 knots, twenty-four tons. She was scrapped in 1879.

The next three steamers, the *Colorado*, *Golden City*, and *Sacramento*, were similar in design, known for long, covered decks to shade first class passengers and provide ventilation. The first, the 3,600-ton, 343-foot by 45-foot *Golden City*, was the finest wooden sidewheeler ever built, and served as the prototype for later Pacific Mail steamers. Master builder Webb finished this ship in August 1863. With both boilers forward of the engine, she had just one squat smokestack for almost 2,000 passengers to view.

Her massive walking-beam engine produced 1,800 horsepower to drive two 40-foot-diameter paddle wheels at ten revolutions per minute, and was capable of 17 knots. Beginning Pacific Mail service on November 3, 1863, the *Golden City* became the most economical ship of the fleet. At 10.5 knots, the ship burned thirty-nine tons of coal a day; at 12 knots, fifty-eight tons. She grounded and broke up in 1870 off of what was then Lower California.

The *Sacramento*, at 2,700 tons, and 304 by 43 feet, joined the fleet in 1864. "Her upper deck, one-sixteenth of a mile long, affords a splendid promenade," a passenger remarked in 1865. Since 1872, the Sacramento Reef off Baja California has marked her remains.[9]

The 3,700-ton, 340-foot *Colorado* came in 1865. Following the Pacific Mail's award of the government mail contract to the Far East, the company partially rebuilt her upper decks and rigging for the inaugural run to Yokohama and Hong Kong on January 1, 1867. She arrived at the first port on January 24, and the second on January 30. Wreckers demolished her in 1879.

SS **GOLDEN CITY** – *William H. Webb's 343-foot **Golden City** marked the height of wooden sidewheel ship design. Entering Pacific Mail service in 1863, she departs San Francisco at a coal-saving 10.5 knots with her name whipping on the foremast flag. Image from the collection of Robert Chandler.*

3

RUNNING A STEAMSHIP IS NOT CHEAP

Mail steamers consistently made the 5,400 nautical mile run from New York to California via Panama in twenty-two to twenty-six days, subjecting passengers to great changes in climate. They dropped from 40 degrees north latitude to 7 degrees north, and then returned to 38 degrees north.

New York to Aspinwall
2,075 nautical miles   8 1/4 knots   10.5 days

Panama to San Francisco via Acapulco
3,275 nautical miles   10 1/8 knots   13.5 days

In comparison, in 1928, steamers took 5.5 days for this Atlantic run, and ten days on the Pacific. Gold Rush ships could steam faster than they did, but the economics of steamer travel dictated naval architecture. Engines, boilers, and 400 tons of coal accounted for forty percent of registered tonnage. Additionally, forty tons of ice, provisions for perhaps 500 passengers with baggage at 100 pounds each, and 300 fifty-five-pound mail bags and 110-pound sacks took room. Such mail steamers could carry only compact valuables — passengers, mail, bullion, express, and high value freight.

All paid a premium to travel, and those equipped with voices complained. Sacramentan William E. Cunningham, Jr., aboard the reliable *Golden Gate* to begin school at Harvard, wrote in his journal on May 14, 1860:

Steam was lessened as the Captain's orders are to arrive at Panama on Friday night [the 18th], and at the rate we have been traveling, we would arrive there a day or two before hand. It is an imposition on passengers when instead of going 300 miles or more as they could do, as they approach nearer the Isthmus, they go slower each day. They could easily make the trip in 11 1/2 days [rather than the usual 13.5 days]. So much for the money making spirit and selfishness of the Company.[10]

Good coal came around Cape Horn, averaging $20 a ton during the 1850s and $11 in the 1860s. Pacific Mail steamers traveled at speeds from 10 to 12 knots, and the two-knot increase made quite a difference in fuel consumption. The *Golden Gate* burned 37.75 tons daily at 10 knots; 12 knots devoured almost double that at 65.25 tons. At a rate of ten knots, and a distance of 240 nautical miles a day, she would burn 520 tons of coal for a typical voyage. At 12 knots and 288 nautical miles a day she used 740 tons for the trip. The *Golden Gate* averaged 254 nautical miles for 13.5 days at 10.6 knots to keep within a daily allotment of forty-five tons of coal, or about 600 tons per voyage.

A several-year mix of company figures gives an approximation of expenses and revenues. In 1855, the average trip to Panama cost $38,000. Outfitting the *Golden Gate* in May of that year cost $19,500; 720 tons of coal at $24 added $17,300, to total $37,000. Average passenger revenues per trip in 1853 were $38,700 and in 1854, $34,500, showing that margins, exclusive of the $7,000 mail subsidy, were close.

SS **SAN FRANCISCO** – *This print made in 1854 by N. Currier of New York has a sad and ironic story with strong Bay Area ties. Built for Pacific Mail in 1853, the ship left New York on her maiden voyage for San Francisco, encountering severe gales off Cape Hattaras, where she foundered. While about 200 lives were lost, some 300 lives were saved by heroic crew members of nearby vessels. One such survivor was Theodore L. Schell, who worked for Pacific Mail, and for whom Schellville (Sonoma County), CA, was later named. After his rescue from one of the worst shipwrecks in U.S. history, he acquired this litho depicting his ordeal, and it remained in his family for more than 150 years. Schell is also interesting because he originally came to California in 1849 aboard the SS* **Panama***, one of the company's earliest Gold Rush steamers. From the collection of Stephen J. and Jeremy W. Potash. Photo by Cathy Forbes.*

In addition, for many years the Pacific Mail bribed Commodore Vanderbilt so that he would not run an opposition line against them; it cost some $2 million over the years. Whenever Vanderbilt thought he could make more, he broke the agreement.

Costs and revenues fluctuated constantly. In 1859, expenses for an outbound trip of the *Golden Gate* had dropped some $4,000 to only $15,700, exclusive of coal. At $11,800 for the *Constitution* in 1862 and the *Sacramento* in 1868, plus, say, $6,600 in coal, a trip cost amounted to $18,500, or almost a $10,000 decrease in the decade.

More travelers headed west than went east. From 1858 to 1867, an average of 11,000 souls annually left California via Panama, compared to 19,000 a year who were arriving. A sampling of passenger revenues from those heading east shows the *Golden Gate* in the summer of 1858 took in $27,400 for one voyage, and the *Sonora* in March 1859 received $13,800.

In October 1862, single voyage receipts dropped to $7,500, and in January 1863, to $5,600. Yet, in April and May 1869, voyages of the *Constitution* and *Colorado* earned $19,500 each, but after the transcontinental railroad went through, dropped to $8,800 and $6,500, respectively in June.

The Pacific Mail struggled to make money, but strong passenger fares brought profitability and allowed the company to grant good dividends to its 500 shareholders. The company paid its first dividend in July 1850, a whopping fifty percent on shares valued at $100 each. Dividends of twenty percent followed until May 1853. Buying out the competition forced suspension of paid-out earnings until May 1856. From then through 1867, the Pacific Mail paid shareholders from ten to thirty percent on their investments. Competition and heavy expense outfitting the China steamers led to no dividend in 1868. The next year brought nine percent, and then nothing until the 1880s.

4

Pay to Ride

Steamship companies charged what the traffic would bear. The U.S. mail contract made the Pacific Mail the standard. New, poorly financed opposition companies with lesser quality steamers and often dubious morals continually sought to undercut.

In 1849, the Pacific Mail sold tickets only to Panama. Passengers arranged transportation the best they could across the Isthmus, and then the Atlantic steamship company had its own fees. In July 1849, Pacific Mail raised first class passage from $250 to $300, and steerage from $100 to $150. Meanwhile, the United States Mail Steamship Company charged an additional $150 and $80 from the Isthmus to New York for these two classes. By December, through fares between San Francisco and New York were $380 and $200.

Through 1851 and 1852, travel ranged from $200–330 for first cabin, $175–290 for second cabin, and $100–200 for steerage. With Cornelius Vanderbilt running by Nicaragua, and other opposition on the Panama route, 1853 saw prices drop to a range of $200–250; $150; and $50–$100 for the three classes.

The Nicaragua route certainly gave the Pacific Mail a run for its money. Between 1852 and 1855, the years of greatest travel on this alternate route, forty percent of the 119,000 arriving passengers and forty-four percent of the 77,000 departing ones chose it. Similarly, twenty-six percent of the $171 million in treasure that departed California during those years traveled by Nicaragua.[11]

No wonder an 1854 song, "Humbug Steamship Companies," had a cynical leer. Its lyrics date it between the first sailing to Panama of Cornelius Vanderbilt's Independent Opposition steamer *Yankee Blade* on June 1, 1854, and its wreck on October 1:

The greatest imposition that the public ever saw,
Are the California Steamships that run to Panama;
They're a perfect set of robbers, and accomplish their
*   designs*
By a general invitation to the people of the mines.

Then come along, come along, you that want to go,
The best accommodations, and the passage very low;
Our boats they are large enough, don't be afraid
The Golden Gate is going down to beat the Yankee
*   Blade.*

They have opposition on the route, with cabins very
*   nice,*
And they advertise to take you for half the usual price;
They get thousands from the mountains, and then deny
*   their bills,*
So you have to pay the prices, or go back into the hills.

In early November 1853, the *Golden Gate* left Panama a half day before the Independent Opposition Line's *Uncle Sam* and came up in twelve days, compared to the *Uncle Sam's* 12.5 days. Songwriter John A. Stone predicted that the Vanderbilt's line's *Yankee Blade* likewise would be slower than Pacific Mail, despite the *Yankee Blade's* handstamped advertisement on envelopes, "Ahead of the Mails."

Stone directed his animus more toward the unscrupulous Vanderbilt than the Pacific Mail:

You are driven round the steerage like a drove
of hungry swine,
And kicked ashore at Panama by the Independent Line;

Companies constantly changed rates. Fares detailed in three issues of the *Alta California* are instructive:

STEAMER RATES

February 16, 1854		July 30, 1854		September 28, 1854

PACIFIC MAIL STEAMSHIP COMPANY
THE MOST SPEEDY AND RELIABLE ROUTE! AHEAD OF ALL OTHER LINES

CALIFORNIA		SONORA		SONORA
Upper Deck Stateroom	$150	Upper Cabin	$275	$150
Dining Saloon	$100	Lower Cabin	$200	$100
Second Cabin	$75	Upper Steerage	$140	$50
Steerage	$50	Lower Steerage	$135	

Note: The new *Sonora*, which arrived May 31, was larger and more luxurious than the 1848 *California*. Passengers could purchase from the agent "Transit Tickets from Panama to Aspinwall (ship to ship) covering all expenses."

INDEPENDENT OPPOSITION, VIA PANAMA
Edward Mills/Cornelius Vanderbilt, September 1853-October 1854
THROUGH AHEAD OF ALL OTHER LINES

UNCLE SAM		YANKEE BLADE		YANKEE BLADE
First Cabin Saloon	$150	Upper Saloon	$275	$175
		Main Saloon	$245	
Second Cabin	$80	Lower Cabin	$200	$150
		Upper Steerage	$140	
Steerage	$50	Lower Steerage	$135	$50

"Through Ticket including Isthmus Transit."

NICARAGUA STEAMSHIP COMPANY
Cornelius K. Garrison and Charles Morgan, April 1853-January 1856
THE SHORTEST, QUICKEST, AND HEALTHIEST ROUTE!

BROTHER JONATHAN		BROTHER JONATHAN		CORTES
Upper Deck Stateroom	$175	Upper Saloon	$275	$200
First Cabin Saloon	$150	Main Saloon	$220	
Second Cabin	$100	Lower Cabin	$200	$150
Steerage	$50	Steerage	$135	$80

Beginning on December 27, 1853, "The only Through Line giving tickets which include the Isthmus Transit."

A steerage ticket for the "Rolling Moses" conveniently has no price. In 1866, the era of this ticket, the Opposition Line charged $50; the Pacific Mail, $100. Shortly, the **Moses Taylor** *accepted steerage passengers for as little as $30. Prices changed voyage by voyage to meet the competition. Although service and conditions were not as good as the Pacific Mail, economy-minded travelers well patronized the Opposition and alternate route. Image from the collection of Robert Chandler.*

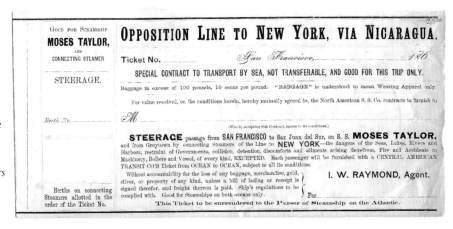

Your baggage is thrown overboard, the like you never saw,
A trip or two will sicken you of going to Panama.[12]

In 1855, both routes charged $300 First Cabin, $250 Second, and $150, Steerage. Spring 1856 saw Pacific Mail fees at $250, $175, and $100, while November brought a drop for the latter two classes to $125 and $50. June 1857 saw a rise to $300, $250, and $150.

The year 1859 brought another of Vanderbilt's opposition lines and, of course, a rate war. The Commodore charged $100, $75, and $50 to go to New York via Panama. Once the rate war was over, in February 1860, the Pacific Mail demanded $200, $150, and $100. The *Alta*, on May 8, 1861, in denying a rumor that the company was going to raise its prices, praised its consistency for almost a year: "The fare has not been changed since last June." In 1862, first cabin was $160 to $200, second cabin, $150, and steerage, $90.

Calculating fares becomes tricky for the remainder of the decade. California remained on the gold standard, making Pacific Coast prices comparable to pre-Civil War prices. The eastern United States accepted U.S. Government currency. In July 1862, depreciation began accelerating and reached a low point of 39 cents on the gold dollar in August 1864. California sources, of course, quoted gold, while New York papers priced fares in inflated greenbacks.

In a circular for the *Golden City* sailing from San Francisco on April 13, 1864, fares were $239 gold for first cabin, outside rooms; $188 for first cabin, inside rooms; $107 for second cabin; and

$60 for steerage. For easterners, that meant $390, $310, $175, and $100 in currency. Similarly, an August 1864 New York first class fare of $400 amounted to only $156 gold.

On February 3, 1864, the opposition paddler *America* sailed from San Francisco to Panama, and 150 of its 550 passengers testified that the competition was "a great benefit." They stated, "The *Opposition Line* has put it within the means of nearly all to make a visit to our friends in the East, and return home to our adopted home in California, without spending a fortune in doing so." Not only was the ship "neat and comfortable," but even steerage passengers enjoyed good food three times a day.

In August 1864, the Central America Transit Company began running regular monthly steamers via the Nicaragua route, and, like the North American Steamship Company, continued on this route until April 1868. Its opposition caused the *Golden City*, sailing on December 13, 1864, to take passengers for $187, $135, and only $48 in steerage. Between 1865 and 1867, the Nicaragua opposition carried 19 percent of the 70,000 arriving in California and 20 percent of the 49,000 leaving.

Early in 1865, the competition began to show. *The San Francisco Directory for the Year Commencing December 1865* listed in its "Chronological History," drawn from the *Alta California*:

March 10, 1865: "The following [gold] rates of fare on the outgoing steamers are lower than have been charged for years.

"P.M.S.Co.: First Cabin, outside stateroom $150; First Cabin, facing dining saloon $115; Second Cabin $70; Steerage $40.

SS **JOHN L. STEPHENS** – *John L. Stephens, an executive of the Pacific Mail Steamship Company, was dispatched to Panama by William Aspinwall after the latter had started the company's Panama-San Francisco line in 1848. His mission was to demonstrate to the traveling public that it would be safe for passengers to cross the Isthmus of Panama from the Atlantic to the Pacific in order to embark on northbound company ships for San Francisco. Stephens failed dismally in his mission because–while in Panama– he died of malaria. The company named this handsome ship, launched in 1852, for him. With construction of the Panama Railway a few years later–also an Aspinwall project–travel across the Isthmus continued to expand and the ship remained in Pacific Mail's Gold Rush service until 1860. Lithograph attributed to George F. Nesbitt & Company, New York, ca. 1852. From the collection of Stephen J. and Jeremy W. Potash. Photo by Cathy Forbes.*

"Opposition: First Cabin $110; Second Cabin $65; Steerage $35." The actual newspaper account added, "Cheap enough."

March 13, 1865: "The GOLDEN CITY and the AMERICA [794 people] left with an unusually large number of passengers, owing to the low rates of fare."

Michael Kelly presented the personal side of a steerage passenger's life in a letter to his wife that day:

San Francisco, March 13, 1865

Dear Wife:

Now, about your Passage. When you receive your money, go to the offices of both the old line and the opposition line if there's any opposition at the time. If you can get your Passage near as cheap on the old line come on it, for it is the best. In case there would be no opposition at the time, it will pay to wait a few weeks if you can find for a certainty that one will run then, for it will make the old line come down with the rate of Passage. They have a Boat leaving from here to day. They carry for fifty dollars in both lines in the steerage, but when there is no opposition, the Passage is one hundred and twenty-eight Dollars.

Be sure and come the old line, and if you have any Money left after your Passage, be sure and Bring either Gold or Silver for Bills are not Worth one cent here. It would be well to Bring one or two Dollars in ten cent Pieces. They are very Handy for change.

You will be Sure and bring a Blanket sheet or Comforter, and you will have to buy a Straw Mattress in New York, for they will not give you any on the Boat. You will be sure on your arrival in New York not to give your Baggage check to any one until you're ready to go to the steamer with it your self. You will Pack the things you will not want to use in your trunk and take the things you will want on the Steamer in your carpet Bag, for they will take your trunk and keep it for some days before you can get at it, and be sure and keep your ticket safe as soon as you engage your Passage ticket. Write the same day overland [expecting this mail would beat the ship] and let me know what steamer you are coming on, and when you arrive in San Francisco stop in the Boat until I will meet you, for you might get in in the Night. Be sure and do as I write.

It will be well for you to take some good Brandy, for you might be sick and you could not get it aboard. Be sure and have a sharp look for your things aboard, for they will steal everything they can get their Hands on.

I am your affectionate Husband,

MICHAEL KELLY

[P.S.] You will be careful and not eat much Fruit at Aspinwall, or sleep on Deck at night, for Panama [Yellow] fever is very easy to take [as mosquitoes spread it]."[13]

Similarly, the New York currency fares of $350, $250, and $125 in September 1865, and $300, $200, and $100 a year later, Californians valued at $241; $172; and $86, and $207, $138, and $69 in gold. "Special Reduced Rates!" for the PMSS *Ocean Queen* leaving New York on November 1, 1866, left first class rates intact, but dropped second cabin and steerage rates down to $150 and $75 currency, or $136 and $68 gold. Children between six and twelve years were one-half fare; from two to six, one-fourth fare, and infants, free.[14]

Yet, after Vanderbilt left the sea in 1865 to go into railroads, another foe surfaced – former friends. In the mid-1860s, Brown Bros., an international investment banking firm, gained control of the Pacific Mail. These bean-counters put return to shareholders above service to customers, and began to transform the Pacific Mail into the low class of its former Atlantic rivals.

In July 1866, a new firm, the North American Steamship Company, succeeded the Central American Transit Company on the Nicaragua and then, on the Panama route. It had shipbuilder William H. Webb as its president, and William Henry Aspinwall was also closely involved. The usual rate war ensued.

That brought immigration, to the *Alta's* delight. "Taking advantage of the extraordinary low rates of fare by steamer to New York since the inauguration of the opposition line via Panama," it said on December 19, 1867,

In 1865, the 314-foot PMSS **Colorado** *steams through a school of porpoises on the Panama run, amusing passengers. From Albert D. Richardson's,* **Beyond the Mississippi.** *Image from the collection of Robert Chandler.*

great numbers of miners and others from the interior, who usually spend the winter season in San Francisco, are going home this winter on a brief visit to relatives and friends at the East. The great majority of the passengers now leaving for the East [319 on the *Constitution*] will return within the next four months, and each one will,

on the average, induce two friends to come here to make a home on the shores of the Pacific.

The Pacific Mail reduced first, second, and third class tickets to $126, $45, and $35 gold, but better was to come. On February 18, 1868, the *Alta* remarked that the rivalry had halved fares "Down to Bed Rock," or $50, $35, and $25. It also pitted paying passengers against coal consumption when it advertised through voyages of 20 to 22 days from San Francisco to New York.

Yet Webb had embarked on a quixotic quest. With the completion of the transcontinental railroad pending, the Pacific Mail threw its energies into trans-Pacific service. In November 1868, Webb closed down the competing firm. In 1869, the Pacific Mail charged $200, $110, and $55, compared to $173 for a railroad trip on a through train from San Francisco to New York.

With the railroad completed, one San Francisco matron fussed, "People here do not seem to think any thing of coming or going by Sea." Instead, she said, they "take rail to save time as they are often business people that go, and every one, I suppose, wants to try the Overland, as it is a new thing." Pacific Mail, though, soon charged half what the railroad did, but as it stopped at many ports to build up coastwise trade, took even longer to reach Panama.[15]

In twenty years, the steamship companies instituted a steady downward spiral in fares. During that time, first class fares dropped as much as $100 to $300 gold—depending on competition for that particular sailing.

5

The Mail Must Go Through!

Carrying the United States mail brought the Pacific Mail Steamship Company and its Atlantic counterpart, the United States Mail Company, into existence. Just as the federal government had done for half a century with stagecoach companies, subsidizing them to build roads and carry the blessings of literacy to outlying frontier settlements, so it did with steamships. William H. Aspinwall's 1848 contract ran for ten years. It first paid $199,000, but ultimately $348,350 annually. As written, it required direct steamer mail to Astoria, Oregon, but the Gold Rush made San Francisco THE Pacific Coast port. On June 19, 1848, Aspinwall received a modification allowing him to supply Oregon by sail until he could acquire small steamships.

On that first voyage, the *California* and its 6,000 letters and additional newspapers took twenty-nine days from Panama to reach San Francisco. After that, for the next ten voyages in 1849, the *California*, *Panama*, and the *Oregon* regularly arrived in twenty-two or twenty-three days. In November the steamer docked with 30,000 letters. Sometimes steamer schedules created friction with timely answers. One Pacific Mail shipping clerk reported to New York on November 1, 1849:

> We have tried hard to keep the Steamers regular on this line and I think we have succeeded very well. Up to the present time, no delay has occurred and although Mr. [Alfred] Robinson [a Californian since 1829, appointed Pacific Mail Steamship Company agent in late 1848] was waited upon last evening by several committees to detain the *California* until Saturday next [November 3] on account of the arrival of the *Panama* last evening with 3 or 4 backmails, and it being impossible to sort such a large number of letters in such a short time, but Mr. R. thought it better that the boat should leave on her appointed day, and she sails this evening with 296 Passengers and $917,000 on her freight list. [She left November 2.] This will start the good folks at home afresh and the steamer for some months to come will be crowded both ways.[16]

However, competition coerced the Pacific Mail. On August 15, 1850, the *Alta California* announced that the two 600-ton, screw-propelled PMSS *Carolina* and the *Columbus* of George Law's Line of Pacific Steamers sailed from San Francisco at 4 P.M.. Law, then the best-known steamer proprietor in the nation, wished to add the Pacific Ocean to his Atlantic Ocean empire. The Post Office closed the mails for the Atlantic states at noon, but the Merchants' Exchange and the *Alta* office each kept a letter bag open until 3 P.M. Both ships arrived at the Isthmus in twenty-one days. In general, Law out-sailed the Pacific Mail until it bought him out the next year. Then, Law and the Pacific Mail kept to their respective oceans.

Furthermore, the San Francisco postmaster allowed Law's opposition ships to carry mail. Although shortly overruled to give the contract

SS **CONSTITUTION** – *Built by William Webb's New York yard for Pacific Mail and launched in 1861, this large ship was chartered out to the War Department at $2,500 per day, according to John Kemble in* **The Panama Route, 1848-1869.** *She then served between Panama and San Francisco from 1862-1869. The lithograph was made by Endicott of New York, ca. 1861. Like the lithograph of the* **Tennessee,** *this print was owned by Renee Pierre Schwerin, who served as vice president and general manager of the company under Collis P. Huntington. From the collection of Stephen J. and Jeremy W. Potash. Photo by Cathy Forbes.*

line an official monopoly, opposition steamship lines merely supplied their own mail bags.

For news-starved Californians, George Law's gumption doubled mail delivery. Beginning on June 18, 1850, his ships sailed mid-month as well as around the first of the month, and although Law did not have the mail contract, his ships carried letters. The Pacific Mail caught on quickly, and when the next mid-month came, the PMSS *Tennessee* sailed on July 15, 1850, and twice-monthly sailings became the norm. At the same time, the government placed mail agents at Panama and aboard the paddlers.

With mail steamers sailing twice a month, a cycle, system, and ethos developed for letter-writing. Writers, particularly at a distance from New York and San Francisco, had to calculate internal mail time, while all had to realize mentally that the steamer would not wait. Furthermore, two months, a month out and one back, symbolized fast communication.

On September 15, 1851, G. Winter and Benjamin G. Latimer, Battery Street commission merchants, wrote to Messrs. Flemming & Douglass in Alexandria, Virginia, by the S.S. *Panama.* The

roundtrip reply to the Virginians took 3 months, 10 days to inform them they had completely miscalculated the California market:

San Francisco, September 15, 1851

Gentlemen:

Your esteemed favor dated July 10th came to hand on 7th inst. only, having laid over at New York until 26th July.

We much regret the loss that was sustained by you in the sale of your segars, but neither at the time they were sold or now could better rates be obtained, and with the winter season rapidly setting in, there is small prospect of improvement ahead.

Stimulated by the high rates obtained for that article in the fall of 1850, shipments have since poured in from every part of the world, and we deemed it wise under the circumstances, thus aware that we were making a heavy loss, to close yours out, and it was only by availing ourselves of the excitement in the market, prevalent after the fire [of May 4], that we succeeded in obtaining the rates returned.

Winter & Latimer's reply made all connections, and arrived in Virginia on October 20, one month, five days after departing San Francisco.[17]

"I wrote you the first steamer after I arrived," a new bride only two and a half months in California wrote her sister in Maine on December 14, 1851, "and the next did not write to any one, was sick."

These details emphasized the yearning for word from homes left behind. She continued,

> I wrote the last steamer to Hannah and this to you, so you see I intend you shall hear from me every steamer.
>
> There has been a mail steamer [*Tennessee*] come in this morning, but we cannot have any letters till ten tomorrow, and the mail closes tonight for New York, and if I have a letter I cannot answer it. I hope I have letters, for I had none this last steamer. You must think of me sometimes.

'ONLY A HEADACHE.'

"Only a Headache" was an excuse heard more often on the rolling Atlantic steamers. "Seasickness claimed me for its victim nearly all the voyage," a woman complained. From Albert D. Richardson's, **Beyond the Mississippi.** *Image from the collection of Robert Chandler.*

A post script quickly followed when the Post Office came through:

> Since I wrote the above, I have received your letter and the steamer [*Panama*] does not take the mail till [7 A.M.] the 16th, and therefore gives me one day more to write.[18]

The long lines of homesick Californians waiting for letters became legendary. San Franciscan S. Lucy wrote a long run-on sentence to his brother in New Hampshire on October 21, 1852:

> After we had ate our breakfast, we went up to the Post-Office after a letter from Edwin, but they were sorting out the mail that came in on the *Golden Gate* and the Office would not be open until 4 O'clock, and then there was such a rush that we did not yet get our letter until 11 O'clock today, but at last we got it, and never, in my opinion, was a seal parted with more anxiety, and a letter read with more joy.[19]

The *Alta* quickly issued an extra edition at 7 A.M. on Wednesday, October 20, 1852, after the ship arrived in thirteen days, nine hours from

Panama [twelve days, four hours running time at 11.25 knots], stating,

> The *Golden Gate* brings a large mail, and 450 passengers, among which are 50 ladies, and 30 children. She brings dates to [September] 23rd. It was healthy on the Isthmus, and the roads in good condition when the *Golden Gate* left.

On February 15, 1854, morning papers proved that accommodation for customers continued. They praised the postmaster for keeping a letter bag open "till within a few minutes before the departure of the steamer" at noon. That same year, the Nicaragua line advertised, "The Mail Bag will close Fifteen Minutes before sailing of the Steamer. All letters free."

When the *John L. Stephens* arrived, steamship company and postmaster delayed mail closing and sailing until 3 P.M. to allow merchants to answer letters. Adams & Co. and Wells, Fargo & Co. would have delivered incoming letters entrusted to them immediately, thereby justifying their higher express rates.

Yet, on September 1, 1854, the result was different. The *Sonora* arrived at 4 P.M. on August 31, with "by far the largest [mail] ever dispatched to the Pacific." Still, the *Alta* declared that "the steamers and mails will leave this morning [at 8 A.M.] as advertised, without any detention on account of the arrival of the Atlantic mails."

Additionally, stationers, book sellers, and news dealers provided an "Only In San Francisco" service. They kept track of steamer sailings for the bewildered. In 1854, the *Alta* remarked that one newspaper stand of many sold 6,000 newspapers on Steamer Day. The paper's unnamed entrepreneur was either Charles P. Kimball, who advertised himself as "The Noisy Carrier," or John W. "Jerry" Sullivan.

The *Alta's* enterprising proprietor knew of last-minute letter writers and kept postage stamps handy in a cardboard box. Kimball and Sullivan were two of several letter bag operators, unique to San Francisco, who for a small fee, delivered bags of letters on time to either the Post Office or the non-contract steamers. "Via Nicaragua Ahead of the Mails" handstamps on letters advertised their reliability.

Isolated easterners and upcountry Californians could become quickly confused on steamer sailings. On November 2, 1853, Prescott Martin wrote from Pomfret, New York, on Lake Erie to his brother Noble in Sacramento about the regularity of mail from California: "Your letter mailed Sept. 30th arrived October 31," he said, adding, "We have got 4 or 5 papers from you and all of your letters straight."

From New York to California was a different matter. "Strange you do not get a letter from home," Prescott said. "We have written you 4 letters before this, [however] we was misinformed when the mail left New York." Even though Noble Martin received this fifth letter, it arrived on January 18, 1854, after 78 days.[20]

In December 1854, an attorney, disappointed that he had not received a letter from his distant wife, ordered "On receiving a letter from me you must write immediately or it may not reach New York in season for the steamer." Actually, even that was not good enough. He expostulated, "Don't wait till mine are received before beginning to write; have the great body of yours written in advance."

That four Prescott Martin letters went missing became all too normal, and their non-arrival emphasizes a significant aspect. Writing letters was a big thing to Americans; correspondence to and from Californians indicates that months would go by between letters. When written, senders wished them delivered.

The same attorney stressed their importance. To his wife in frozen Vermont, he wrote on December 14, 1854,

> I never liked to write letters very well till since I left home; but there is no calculating and no expressing the keen yet quiet pleasure it now gives me. It really seems if I was with you again amid the walls of home, talking, laughing, reading, singing, or sitting with my feet on the wood-box.[21]

The Post Office, however, made no guarantees of delivery. Until April Fool's Day 1855, American writers had the choice of sending their missives pre-paid or collect. The vast majority of mail went collect, as senders refused to throw away money. Once delivered, the rejoicing recipient paid.

In the east, local U.S. rates stabilized at 5 cents collect and 3 cents prepaid per half ounce; from August 14, 1848, until July 1, 1851, Gold Rush Californians paid 12.5 cents. However, long distance steamer mail to and from California, by a law of March 3, 1847, cost eight times the eastern collect rate. When the Pacific Mail began deliveries, the government charged 40 cents, paid or collect. On July 1, 1851, it reduced this rate for over 3,000 miles to 6 cents prepaid and 10 cents collect.

April 1, 1855 brought mandatory prepayment and "general dissatisfaction" in California over the price charged. Required prepaid postage to and from the east jumped 67 percent from 6 cents to 10 cents! It was "an oppression" and "an unjust burthen," the *Alta* stormed. On the next Steamer Day, stationer Louis H. Bonestell was typically behind. On April 16, he wrote home, "I have no time to write, but will scratch off a few lines." However, his wife refused to write, due to the high postage. "She considers it an outrage and will not patronize Uncle Sam on account of it."[22]

Putting the best face on the situation, the *Alta* remarked on May Day 1855, "It is believed that this new law will not long remain in force." The paper was correct – but only if eight years is considered a short time. To reward California's Civil War patriotism, on July 1, 1863, all domestic letters cost three cents per half ounce. The Ernest A. Wiltsee Collection on the mezzanine level of the Wells Fargo History Museum in San Francisco exhibits fine examples of all Gold Rush rates and markings.

Californians, with less excuse, had problems equal to easterners in judging steamer sailing dates. The personality of Ephraim Cutting in Murphys made him too cheap to send his letters by express to San Francisco. Cutting therefore complained on December 21, 1851, "I am obliged to write a week previous to the Steamer's starting." The next year, still refusing to pay for timeliness, he confessed on July 19, 1852, that he had missed a mailing "through my foolish carelessness in making calculations for the Steamer's departure from San Francisco."[23]

Living in San Francisco made the task no easier. Joseph Witner wrote to one of his sisters on December 5, 1858: "I only know that 'Steamer day' always comes around before I am ready for it, and that my writing is postponed, until no longer delays are allowable and then all is hurry and confusion, and what 'I wish' must wait for what 'I must.' In this way the claims of my dear Sisters are delayed until months intervene between my letters." His letter was in one of 110 bags that sailed on the *Golden Age*.[24]

In January 1858, James M. Hutchings described San Francisco Post Office operations in his *California Magazine*. In eighty trips from August 21, 1854, to December 16, 1857, 24,150 mail bags arrived in an average of 25.25 days from New York – only three days longer than the part-way voyage from Panama to San Francisco in 1849. The reliable *Golden Age*, *Golden Gate*, *John L. Stephens*, and *Sonora* docked averaging 302 bags of mail on each ship with a total of 35,000 letters per trip.

However, Californians could not match this incoming production. The eighty departing trips carried 8,856 bags, or about one-third of the number that arrived. In 1854, eight departures averaged 101 bags. That figure dropped to ninety-six bags in the depression year of 1855, and then averaged 110 bags a trip in 1856 and 1857 – excluding the exciting, tumultuous Vigilance Committee Summer. From May 21 to September 5, 1856, the *John L. Stephens*, *Golden Age*, and *Sonora* averaged 140 bags each on eight trips.

Partial records from December 1859 to November 1860 show pattern continuation. Of twenty-seven arrivals, eighteen ships sailed in between twenty-two and twenty-four days from New York, cutting off a day-and-a-half from mid-1850s time. From December 1859 through March 1860, over 260 bags came in with each steamer

William H. Hudson, captain of the PMSS **Sacramento**, *sailed on April 13, 1865, with this letter safe in Wells, Fargo & Co's letter bag. On May 5, 23 days later, it arrived in New York. Merchants preferred the tried and true route by sea rather than turmoil and uncertainty by land– but to be safe, sent duplicate letters by both routes. Image from the collection of Robert Chandler.*

during the winter months; from April through November, after converting trimonthly arrivals to semi-monthly ones, bags ranged from 341 to 438. Departing steamers regularly carried away 90 to 100 or more mail bags, but the bag tally bore little relationship to the number of letters. From December 1859 to June 1860, leaving letters numbered monthly from 56,000 in January 1860 to 33,000 in June of that year. The figures for July are missing, but then August departures dropped to 18,000; September numbered 24,500, and October, only 18,400. Perhaps the decrease is not seasonable, but illustrates the popularity of the Overland Mail.[25]

On September 20, 1859, the *John L. Stephens* carried away the last mail of the original contract. The *Alta* praised the Pacific Mail for its "prompt and safe manner." For a decade "they have not lost a single mail." The wily Vanderbilt then finagled a contract extension to July 1, 1860, and subcontracted the Pacific portion to the Pacific Mail. Creative financing by the Post Office Department

extended this arrangement to June 30, 1861, when the daily Overland Mail went into operation. Heavy and bulky printed material still arrived by sea, and Californians had the option to write "Steamer" on their letters so that the post office would direct them that way. For years, merchants sent two copies of letters, one overland and the other by sea.

San Franciscans, though, did not forget their old life line. Nostalgically, Emma Libby wrote to her mother in Maine on September 29, 1863: "I hear the old steamer Gun. I wonder if I shall get a letter in the morning. That is what I always think when I hear it."[26]

Two years later, astute newspaper reporter Albert D. Richardson observed the departure side of mail service as he sailed December 19, 1865, on the *Sacramento*. "'Steamer Day is still a great event," he found. "Everybody spends the night before writing letters; and for the last hour, one or two thousand persons crossed the decks of the departing vessel."[27]

Letter-writers had to judge steamer sailings. San Franciscan Wells wrote to his wife on January 31, 1855, but delayed getting it to the Post Office until after the **John L. Stephens** *had sailed on February 1. A large "Too Late" handstamp recorded its fate. Collection of Robert J. Chandler.*

6

STAGECOACHES BRING COMPETITION: THE OVERLAND MAIL

In the late 1850s, settlement, growing population, and technology challenged and then vanquished the steamer monopoly. In September 1858, the twenty-four-day, semi-weekly Overland Mail stagecoach route by way of Texas and Los Angeles began running. Attorney Oscar L. Shafter wrote October 19 to his father in Vermont about the new institution: "The last time [it] beat the steamer from New York by forty-eight hours. The people here are half frantic with joy. We feel *nearer* to our old homes." By 1860, stagecoaches carried more letters than the semi-monthly steamers.[28]

Stagecoaches had more opportunity than steamers: eight times a month, compared to two. Mails left San Francisco at 1 P.M. on Mondays and Fridays, and beginning January 23, 1860, the Post Office sent all mails overland, via Los Angeles, unless marked "Via Panama." Stagecoaches shaved a few days off steamer mail time and reliably went through in contract time.

With a new mail contract and the secession of the southern states in early 1861, the mail route shifted from the southwest to one running between Placerville, Salt Lake City, and St. Joseph/Atchison. The Republican-dominated Congress also mandated a daily mail, excluding Sundays, to begin on July 1, 1861. The contract was not particularly stringent. It called for twenty days delivery between Placerville and St. Joseph in summer, and twenty-five days during four winter months.

Actual delivery between San Francisco and New York took four days longer. To the stagecoach overland route was added a day by steamboat, railroad, and more stagecoach from San Francisco to Placerville, while on the eastern end, railroads brought letters from St. Joseph into New York in three days. Contract letter times then became twenty-four and twenty-nine days, longer than the Mail Steamers! Of course, the Overland Mail left twenty-six times a month compared to two, so even with delays, letters arrived earlier than most steamer sailings.

The *Alta* remarked on July 19, 1862, "Every letter not marked 'per steamer,' is to be sent overland," for Californians liked the Overland Mail. It was, as the *Alta California* and *Sacramento Union* remarked in the fall of that year, "a faithful and regular institution," delivering mail within twenty to twenty-one days, compared to twenty-four to twenty-five days by steamer. The Overland Mail often cut a week off contract time.

Yet, those sturdy steamers remained ready resources. "I never thought much of the Overland route," Ephraim Cutting grumbled at Murphys, "the Steamer Line was a sure shot." Through the 1860s, the Pacific Mail remained that "sure shot." During times of long disruption from weather to Indian wars, it carried the letter mail just as it transported heavy, bulky, printed material. 1864 showed what the Pacific Mail could do. For several months at a time the postmaster general ordered mails sent by sea.[29]

On January 4, 1864, San Francisco postmaster Samuel H. Parker complained to Washington, "Ordinarily the steamers make the time in twenty-

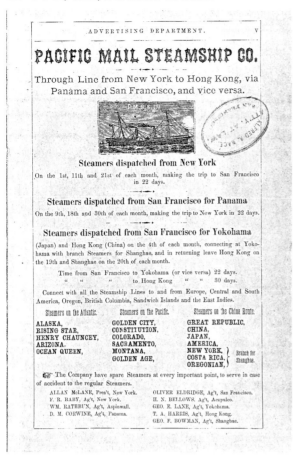

A Pacific Mail advertisement from December 1869 details its extensive routes from San Francisco to New York and Asia carried out by a fleet of 18 steamships built in the 1860s. Image from the collection of Robert Chandler.

four days and when opposition is on, in twenty days, and will continue to beat the overland mail, causing nearly all the business part of the community to patronize the Express [by sea] instead of the mails." Parker tapped a subtle change since the 1850s. Now that lost mails were a rarity, Californians demanded speed as well as safe delivery.[30]

A sampling of docketed envelopes, letters, and newspaper articles from 1864 tells the story:
- Salem, Masssachusetts, January 1, 1864, overland to San Francisco, February 3; thirty-four days.
- Callicoon Depot, New York, January 13, 1864, to Ione City, Nevada, February 27; forty-six days.
- Three Rivers, Michigan, February 14, 1864, to Auburn, California, March 14, thirty days.

- Mining secretary Leslie B. Wooster, San Francisco, March 6, 1864, to his mother:

    Yours of the 17th January and Hat's letter of the 1st of February came to hand the same day [over 30 days for both]. There has been a deal of trouble about the mails this winter, on account of so much snow having fallen east of the Sierras as to blockade the road for weeks. For three weeks we did not receive any overland mail at all.

- San Francisco, May 20, 1864, to Lacon, Illinois, June 18; thirty days.
- San Francisco, July 30, 1864, to Atchison, Kansas, October 5; sixty-eight days during an Indian war.
- San Francisco, September 29, 1864, the *Golden Age* arrived with the back mails, "the largest ever received on the Pacific Coast," according to the *Alta*. The ship brought 70,000 letters, 40,000 for San Francisco, and 30,000 for elsewhere on the Pacific Coast.
- New York September 26, 1864, to San Francisco, October 21; twenty-six days.
- Duquoin, Illinois, October 1, 1864, to Gold Hill, Nevada; twenty-three days.
- Ionia, Michigan, October 28, 1864, to You Bet, Nevada County, October 28; thirty-nine days.
- New York, November 10, 1864, to San Francisco, December 10; thirty-one days.

A summing up came from a San Francisco son to a New York City father: "Your welcome letters of December 20, 1864 and January 3, 1865, came to hand on the 30th of January [forty-two and twenty-eight days], so you can see there is no use of making any calculations on the mails."

On May 8 1865, the San Francisco *Evening Bulletin* complained that Overland letters crossed the plains in thirty-five to forty days.[31]

In 1867, another Indian war broke out. Between April and August, hostile horse-heisting Indians stole 350 animals, burned twelve stations and three stagecoaches, and killed thirteen employees. Again, the reliable steamers took over. Regardless of conditions on the Overland route, good or bad, as Postmaster Parker remarked, Wells Fargo always sent a Letter Express by each steamer. Merchants demanded it.

By 1868, with conditions calmer and the railroad closer, Overland mail came more rapidly. On November 16, a well-off attorney's wife sat down in her parlor at Kearny and Chestnut streets to write her New York City sister, remarking that her letter of October 21 had "come overland, and thus anticipating the Steamer by several days." Two pages later she wrote,

> The mail steamer [*Golden City*] is just coming in, and has passed so closely that one might almost imagine it would be an easy matter to converse with those on board. She seems quite crowded, so that it does not look as though the earthquake [of October 21] has frightened people from seeking a home among us.

In 1868, Pacific Mail steamers had to rescue the Post Office in another way. Congress anticipated the rapid completion of the transcontinental railroad early within the time of the normal four-year mail contract. Therefore, it ordered that beginning October 1, 1868, all printed material would go overland.

This demand increased the weight of westbound mails six times! For the first nine days in October 1868, the New York post office sent a daily average of 660 pounds of letter mail in twelve locked pouches and 3,808 pounds of printed matter in thirty-four sacks. The release of a new issue of *Harper's Monthly* on October 7 and 8 skewed the average when it added fifty sacks weighing over three tons. After a jarring, abrasive ride in a stagecoach, one San Francisco newsdealer lost $11,000 "all chewed up" magazines, which he then "sold to Chinamen for wrapping paper."

Acting on such complaints from San Francisco, the Postmaster General telegraphed to New York on October 24, 1868, "Forward by steamer all mail matter for the Pacific coast which the senders may desire to forward by that route." He broadly included letters as well as publications.[32]

The railroad changed everything. About five months after its completion, on October 4, 1869, Tehama rancher George L. Eastman complained "within three months, the times have changed." Post-railroad conditions were "harder here now than ever." Yet, that railroad speeded mail delivery, and his letter arrived quickly in Springfield, Illinois, on October 12. Average time from San Francisco to New York, the Postmaster General reported, was seven days and two hours.

To show what railroads really could do, the Post Office instituted special mail trains. On June 4, 1876, the press reported, "Arrival of the fast mail train from New York, in 83 hours, 59 minutes, and 16 seconds, with Jarratt & Palmer's theatrical company and guests." The train arrived forty-four seconds short of three-and-a-half days.[33]

*During the Civil War, Confederate commerce raiders decimated Union shipping. Fearing that one might capture an eastbound gold-laden steamer just as the C.S.S. **Alabama** had caught the westbound **Ariel** on December 7, 1862, Wells Fargo offered shippers a choice of rates for treasure. Wells Fargo insurance plus war risk was 5 percent. The cheapest Wells Fargo alternative was "to take your chances and sue the Rebs if they got the steamer." Commission merchant C.H. Strybing chose the alternative (at 0.01785 percent) for his 100-ounce bar that sailed aboard the Orizaba on March 13, 1864. Image from the collection of Robert Chandler.*

7

WELLS FARGO & CO.'S EXPRESS LEADS

On March 18, 1852, Henry Wells, William G. Fargo, and others allied with the American Express Company formed Wells, Fargo & Co.'s Express to perform banking, rapid movement of valuables, and letter delivery on the Pacific Coast. When it opened for business on July 13, 1852, Wells Fargo went head-to-head with Adams & Co., a prominent eastern express that had been an Argonaut of 1849. Adams & Co., the largest and most extensive Pacific Coast express, performed similar services ably until its demise in February 1855.

In October 1852, Wells, Fargo & Co.'s Express advertised that due to "advantageous arrangements," it would "forward Gold Dust, Bullion, Specie, Packages, Parcels & Freight, of all kinds, to and from New York and San Francisco," which would be "in charge of our own messenger through to destination." It added, "Treasure & small parcels, received for shipment up to the latest moment before the departure of the Steamers."[34]

Once aboard ship, the company had specific instructions for its messenger:

Office of Wells, Fargo & Co.
82 Broadway, New York
April 27, 1855

W.B. Latham, Jr.
WF & Co's Messenger per *Northern Light*.

Dear Sir:
    You will have charge of our Express matter this day for San Francisco by Nicaragua route.

Our [101 boxes of] *goods* will be under Bill of Lading from New York to San Francisco. You will have no *direct* charge of them, further than to urge them on when you consider it necessary to do so, but at the same time be careful not to interfere with the Company's officers.

You are furnished by us on leaving here, with a list of all our Express goods going with you and also of all the Trunks and Bags *in your immediate charge* of which Trunks and Bags you will *take especial care* until you arrive at San Francisco and deliver the same *only* to persons connected with our office there.

You are furnished with Custom House Manifests of our Express goods, which you will *be sure* to get properly endorsed by the United States Consular Agent both at San Juan del Norte and San Juan del Sur.

Take no packages from others either here or on the route unless for Consuls or officers of the Steamship Company.

In no case nor under any consideration whatever, let any package, or letter or letters which we have put under your *immediate charge* go out of your care until you deliver the same to persons connected with our San Francisco office as after herein directed.

While on way up on Pacific side, prepare a careful alphabetical list of all San Francisco (City) Letters in your Bag, make it on the headed sheets we give you (dating each sheet.) Get the Purser's Report and put it and your letter list in Letter Bag, and when nearing San Francisco, our News Boat (with Flag and Capt. Martin on board) will come off [from Meiggs' Wharf]. Then throw Bag Letters and Bag Newspapers to him: Be ready for him so as not to miss him. [From the wharf, horses would race into the city.]

Report yourself with Trunks as soon as possible to our folks in San Francisco. Look for our wagon on the dock and go up in it, losing no time.

After eastbound passengers boarded the PMSS **Arizona** *at Aspinwall, they could not leave. Workers met a second Panama Railroad train heavy with treasure. For two hours, they lugged silver bars, bagged gold bars, and boxed coin to the steamer's treasure room. From Albert D. Richardson's* **Beyond the Mississippi.** *Image from the collection of Robert Chandler.*

During any affrays on board ship, remain neutral as far as possible.

Distribute newspapers to Steamer's Officers, Consuls, and respectable passengers you may meet coming this way on Isthmus.

Wishing you a pleasant trip and good health,

We remain Yours,
WELLS, FARGO & CO.
By: Jesse Payne.

P.S. *Be sure* to have *all the bags of newspapers on deck,* ready for immediate delivery on arrival in the Bay of San Francisco.[35]

Latham, however, did not have an easy trip. On May 6, 1855, the Nicaragua steamer *Sierra Nevada* picked up the *Northern Light's* 847 passengers at San Juan del Sur, and sailed on May 11. The Pacific, though, was not pacific. The ship "met with incessant gales from the N.W., with tremendous head seas, retarding her arrival at least two days." Captain James H. Blethen put into San Francisco at 11 A.M. Saturday, May 26, 1855.

Having shipments "in charge of a Special Messenger on EACH STEAMER" brought rewards. One hurried and harried San Franciscan wrote to his congressman on June 5, 1856, as the *Golden Age* prepared to cast off lines, "The mail is closed. I have to send this by Express."[36]

Of course, he had to pay an extra ten cents for this extra care. The federal government allowed Wells Fargo to run its Letter Express only if all letters were enclosed in U.S.-stamped envelopes. The government postal monopoly gained its fee even though it never handled this mail. Since August 1855, Wells Fargo had sold ten-cent U.S. envelopes for the Atlantic states for twenty cents. Wells Fargo's letter bag stayed on board the Panama steamers through the 1860s and beyond.

Turning to packages, Wells Fargo handled two classes of freight crossing the Isthmus. Fast Freight went from one ship on the Atlantic over the railroad to the connecting steamer on the Pacific. Slow Freight took its time across the Isthmus and waited two weeks for the next steamer sailing to San Francisco. To aid merchants, Wells Fargo arranged with New York customs officials to clear 8,000 packages at a time. At the Isthmus, Wells Fargo employees put all small boxes into protective, locked packing trunks, watched by a messenger.

In 1859, rival Freeman & Co.'s Express tried to acquire Sacramento dry goods merchant Charles Crocker's fast freight. He gave Freeman a trial — but stayed with Wells Fargo. "On the arrival of the last steamer," Freeman's Sacramento agent wrote President John Freeman in New York, Crocker

expected goods by our route, but they came by Wells, Fargo & Co., and Crocker says for the following reason: The [Crocker] agent [in New York] called on Freeman & Co. three days prior to the sailing of the steamer and tendered his cases. He was told the steamer was full and was advised to have them kept till the sailing of the opposition [steamer] some days after. This he declined doing, crossed the street, shipped them by Wells, Fargo & Co., and out they came in the steamer which Freeman & Co. thought too full.[37]

By 1865, Wells Fargo's efficiency under General Agent Louis McLane led

to control of half of the steamship's freight business. McLane's brother Allen, president of the Pacific Mail, took notice, and made Wells Fargo "sole Freight Agents of the Pacific Mail S.S. Co., and for the Panama R.R. Co." On December 9, 1865, two days after the first advertisement appeared, the *Colorado* left San Francisco with Wells Fargo's first authorized Pacific Mail freight. Its five percent commission brought Wells Fargo about $80,000 on $1.6 million of business for the year ending September 1, 1867. On February 8, 1869, Pacific Mail advertised it again handled its own freight.

As freight agent, Wells Fargo had an explosive impact on San Francisco one day in 1866. On April 16, in the courtyard of the Parrott Building at the northwest corner of Montgomery and California streets, Wells Fargo employees examined a wooden crate containing a leaking carboy (a large glass bottle in a crate used for shipping corrosive liquids). A requisitioned chisel removed more than the box top.

SILVER TUREEN – Literally every ship in the company's early Gold Rush service called at Panama, where one man was responsible for developing the trade, selling the tickets, maintaining the ships, and keeping westbound passengers calm after their rough crossing of the Isthmus or in event the vessel was held up. That man, who in 1849–in the midst of the travel surge–was appointed General Agent for Pacific Mail with responsibility for the company's steamers, was Capt. William C. Stout. We are still hunting for more information about Capt. Stout, but we do know that in 1853, possibly upon his retirement, this extraordinary covered sterling tureen was presented to him by the company. Made in New York by silversmiths Wood & Hughes (and possibly ordered by PMSS President William Aspinwall, himself) it is inscribed in elegant script:
"Presented to W C Stout – By the Commanders
of the PMSS Co. Steamers – Dec. 1853."
From the collection of Stephen J. and Jeremy W. Potash. Photo by Richard Langs.

Unmarked nitroglycerin exploded with a huge roar, killing a dozen people. Among the dead were Wells Fargo's banker, Samuel Knight, and his predecessor, assayer and supervisor of the Eighth Ward, Gerritt W. Bell. The Wells Fargo History Museum at 420 Montgomery Street displays pieces of a silver service crunched into its packing crate that stood next to the carboy.

All knew Wells Fargo for the gold it moved, and wartime brought complications. Confederate commerce raiders prowled the seas and on December 7, 1862, in the Atlantic, the *Alabama* stopped the mail steamer *Ariel* headed toward the Isthmus. Hardly had the shock waves died away from that incident when Pacific Coast authorities on March 15, 1863, stopped the *J.M. Chapman*, a Confederate privateer, from leaving the San Francisco harbor to prey on the gold-laden sidewheelers.

Since 1862, California gold shippers had played it safe, sending gold from Aspinwall to England and then back to New York under the neutral British flag. Now, bills of lading carried a standard disclaimer, "Not responsible for seizure by privateers or letters of marque, passenger risings on board, etc." In San Francisco, the Army's Provost Guard checked departing steamers, while on the Atlantic, warships escorted the treasure-laden sidewheelers.

On March 4, 1864, Portland hardware merchant Henry W. Corbett wrote from San Francisco to his New York agent:

> I forwarded, as I wrote to you on the 2nd, per Wells, Fargo & Co., $3,000 in gold Coin which I hope will reach you safely. I also forwarded you notes for delivery in a letter per Wells, Fargo & Co., which I was obliged to entrust to a Policeman to deliver to the Express Messenger, as they would not let any one go on board the Steamer [*Golden City*] on the morning she sailed [March 3, 1864] except passengers, they fearing that there was some concerted plan to take this Steamer by certain parties, she having a large amount of Treasure on board, over two million it is said.

Besides a newly-mounted, rifled Parrott cannon that fired a 100-pound shot on the foredeck, 20 soldiers from the Provost Guard sailed on the ship to and from Panama.[38]

Three months later, L. Ware, Jr., wrote playfully of the still tight restrictions, such as those that enabled Wells Fargo to aid Corbett. On June 8, he "went down on the [Folsom Street] wharf to witness the arrival and landing of the passengers from the Steamer *Constitution* from Panama." At 9 A.M. Commodore James T. Watkins docked his ship carrying 852 passengers thirteen days, six hours from the Isthmus. Foremost aboard were Supreme Court Justice Stephen J. Field and his wife, but cabin passengers included a great number of women — and undoubtedly a good number of draft-dodgers.

"I felt quite like an old resident," Ware continued. Due to wartime security,

> those without tickets now kept from boarding the steamer, and the folks on the wharf were constantly crying out to those on the steamer, 'How are your [depreciated] Greenbacks!' 'O! You'll be drafted as soon as you land!' And seeing a Californian pressing through the crowd & shake hands with some pretty sister, cousin, or friend, the cry would be (if he didn't do it), 'Why don't you kiss her?' Altogether they make quite a time of it.[39]

In 1865, with the March 13 sailing of *Golden City*, the *Alta* noticed "Change in the Gold Drift." With this trip, seventy percent of the $1,150,000 treasure aboard went to New York rather than to England.

8

SAILING ALONG
WITH PACIFIC MAIL

Low estimates indicate a half million people were coming to California by steamer between 1849 and 1869, and 300,000 were leaving during the same period. People at both ends were important; the trip itself was not especially significant. Life aboard steamers was to be endured and not written about. Accounts are scarce.[40]

Men for the most part went east on business and returned. They tolerated travel as one of those things that could not be changed. In the 1750s, that might be two months sailing the Atlantic Ocean between the Old and New Worlds; in the 1850s, two weeks; in the 1950s, half a day; and now, only five hours. Go to any airport to realize that while flight time has lessened, complaints have not.

For those in the 1850s heading west via the Isthmus, the time to California doubled the two-week Europe transit to a month, and going both

Crafted by San Francisco silversmith William K. Vanderslice, this goblet is a rare example of presentation silver bearing the name of a pioneer California steamer. It is inscribed:
"Presented to Capt. W.H. Parker by Passengers on Board
STEAMSHIP SACRAMENTO
Jany. 1st, 1869."
This is the same Capt. Parker of Civil War fame, who later captained Pacific Mail ships. The side-wheeler **Sacramento** *was launched in 1863 for the company's Panama-San Francisco service.*
Collection Stephen J. and Jeremy W. Potash.

ways between New York and San Francisco meant two months at sea. Shipboard life became a routine necessity. Attorney Oscar Shafter wrote from the *North Star* on the Atlantic on October 24, 1854, "the larger proportion of the male passengers is made up of old Californians who are going back with their families." One woman wrote on July 19, 1857, from Tehama County to her Amador sister: "I did not have a very pleasant trip a going to the states, but we had quite a pleasant time coming back." That is all she wrote.

Why did she go? To see her parents. She elaborated much more, but in general, "I found them all at home pretty much as we left them, only I found Mother very much changed. She looks so old." With two daughters across the continent, gone from her life, well she might.

The joy of arrival encompassed all. On October 4, 1855, Shafter wrote wife Sarah just before her sailing to meet him after a two-year absence. When the ship came in, he would be standing at "the head of the pier" wearing a white sombrero, and her party was to wave three white handkerchiefs from the upper deck at the stern. Upon recognition, "I shall remove the sombrero aforesaid from the head aforesaid and swing it as mortal man never swung hat before."[41]

Trips were monotonous. The Reverend William C. Mosher wrote home in 1861: "I need not describe to you our voyage for there is a similarity between all voyages to California. We sailed from New York November 21st [1860] and reached San Francisco, December 15th, having had a pleasant passage most of the time."[42]

Longer statements give more of an idea of shipboard life. In 1860, William E. Chamberlain left Sacramento to go to Harvard. To pass time aboard the *Golden Gate*, he kept a journal, which contained an apologetic note, for the beat from the paddlewheels went on, and on, and on:

> I will ask that you will excuse this very poor writing as it is almost impossible for anyone to write so long as the Steamer is in motion. Now she pitches this way, now that; now ploughs her way through the sea and now nicks some wave; now rolling on this side, and now on that.

Extracts from his journal follow:

SATURDAY, MAY 5, 1860.

About 10 A.M. [with $1,130,000 treasure on board] we were slowly moving toward the "Heads." We passed the fort, and soon lost sight of San Francisco. The sea begins to grow rougher, the vessel rolls and pitches and we are on the ocean. Determined, if possible, to avoid sea-sickness, I began to walk the deck with rapid strides, scarcely stopping until night brought her welcome messenger.

SUNDAY, MAY 6, 1860.

After a night's rest, I arose feeling somewhat refreshed although too dizzy to eat my breakfast. Again I sought the deck and wearied with walking, sat down and watched the waves with their snow-white caps.

About noon, we found that since leaving San Francisco, we had gone 260 miles, or 10 miles an hour. Thus far, we have had very pleasant weather, and the prospect bids fair that it will continue. Feeling a little better, I was able to eat some supper. I spent the evening in reading. We have been in sight of land all the time.

MONDAY, MAY 7, 1860.

I woke at 6, and took my morning walk. Felt much better. Had some little appetite for breakfast. We saw about 30 [California Gray] whales and also a few porpoises, gulls and boobies.

TUESDAY, MAY 8, 1860.

To day, I was really surprised to witness the discipline among the waiters; every thing is as regular as clock-work. Their uniformity would be a credit to any body of men. No one can judge unless they have personal observation of their action. The steward with his bell regulates their motions. We have 3 meals daily—breakfast at 8 1/2; lunch at 12, and Supper at 4 1/2 [the first cabin schedule].

FRIDAY, MAY 11, 1860.

To day about 4 o'clock, we slowly made our way to Acapulco. It was really amusing to witness the endeavors of the natives to sell their fruits &c. No sooner had the Steamer come to her stopping place than she was surrounded by small boats containing natives, oranges, limes, bananas, apples, pine-apples, water-melons, cocoa-nuts, eggs, chickens and shells. It was in vain that the officers of the Steamer endeavored by throwing water from a force pump to drive the natives away.

While the water was on one side, the natives were on the other, so finally they were allowed to sell their fruits and shells, and dive for money.

We did not land, as the yellow fever had the previous day numbered 5 Americans among its victims. After about two hours spent in taking in water and coal, we said adieu to Acapulco and slowly made our way out of the harbor and were again on our voyage. Land was in sight all day.

SATURDAY, MAY 12, 1860.

Nothing of much importance occurred to day, excepting in the evening, when we had singing. Among the songs were those that are so dearly cherished, yet which now recall sad feelings, viz: "Home, Sweet Home," "Good News From Home," "Oft in the Still Of Night;" "Remember Thy Mother." These showing what thoughts were uppermost in their minds.

WEDNESDAY, MAY 16, 1860.

This morning, we were the happy recipients of a rain-shower, "Short and sweet," lasting about 15 minutes. At 3, the *John L. Stephens* passed in sight of us, about 15 miles to the west. She was too far for us to exchange signals. We had considerable sport on this account.

Our First Mate, who is full of fun, declared that he saw signals, which he read to the passengers collected near him. I took notes of a few of these, viz: "[John C.] Breckinridge has been nominated as President; Jo Lane as Vice President" [as did happen that June]; "[President James] Buchanan has been assassinated, as also [Emperor] Napoleon [III of France];" "The ship *Adriatic* with 780 souls wrecked near Southampton;" "[Edward] Bates [of Missouri, afterwards Attorney General] nominated by Republicans for President;" "Grand fight between [heavy weight champions, the Benicia Boy, John C.] Heenan and [English champion Tom] Sayers postponed [fought to a draw on April 17, at Farnborough, Hampshire]" &c. The mate was so sober when he made these statements that for some time many of the passengers thought he really was reading the signals.[43]

In 1863, Noyes S. Palmer, the San Francisco agent for the Charter Oak Life Insurance Company, described his long trip of sixteen days, eleven hours up the Pacific Coast. This followed a ten-day trip on the *Ocean Queen*, which sailed Friday, May 23, 1863, making twenty-nine days total. The *Ocean Queen* was a 2,800-ton, 327 foot Vanderbilt steamer built in 1859, with a 42-foot beam and 38-foot paddlewheels.

SAN FRANCISCO, JUNE 20, 1863.
Dear Father:

I arrived in this City yesterday at about 1 O'clock P.M. & was right glad I assure you to find myself on land once more. The trip has been entirely free from storms. The wind was quite fresh on the Atlantic side in crossing the Caribbean Sea [on the *Ocean Queen*] and again on the Pacific side in crossing the Gulf of Tehuantepec. We also had a good breeze during the last 3 days on the Pacific, but no storm. This is certainly the most favorable season of the year for making a trip to California.

On Monday night of June 1st, a little before midnight, we made the light at Aspinwall (previous to this, however, had been in sight of land for several hours). From midnight until daylight we laid off & on waiting for day. Early in the morning we landed at Aspinwall, a small dilapidated town which has recently suffered severely from fire. Many of the children here go entirely naked & some of the men wear no shirts, but only a pair of pantaloons & a hat. A gentleman who has crossed here several times & been delayed on two occasions several weeks, tells me that when he first visited the Isthmus all the children of both sexes and many of the men were seen entirely destitute of clothing of any kind, but coming in contact with civilized people of late years has remedied this & now no adults are seen without clothing of some kind.

We took breakfast in Aspinwall at the City Hotel and were required to pay $1 in gold or silver or $2 in Greenbacks. The rainy season was just commencing. There were frequent showers in which the rain fell for a few minutes in torrents & then the sun would show itself & make it excessively hot. Fresh Oranges, Pineapples, Cocoanuts & Limes in abundance.

At 9 O'clock in the morning we left Aspinwall and crossed the Isthmus (47 miles) in about 4 hours & immediately were taken by a little steamer on board the *Orizaba*, which was to carry us to San Francisco. Our baggage, together with the "fast freight" was brought on afterwards in another train, and we did not get started until about 1 O'clock at night [on June 3]. Our trip across the Isthmus on the Cars was very pleasant, the motion of the Cars producing a little breeze. There were 3 or 4 little villages on the line of the Rail Road, in each of which there was one good house and the other buildings were miserable little huts of the half civilized natives.

Almost every night since we left Panama, the bright phosphorescent light has been seen sparkling in the Ship's wake. I have been surprised that so few vessels have been seen. We have passed 2 steamers and I believe one sailing vessel, tho' I did not see it. We have run close to the Coast, been in sight of land almost every day. An Episcopal clergyman was on board & we have had religious services every Sunday.

On the 10th of June at about 4 A.M. we arrived at Acapulco, Mexico, where we stopped & left some freight, coaled & took on a fresh supply of provisions. The harbor there is the most complete I ever saw. The water is both close in shore & it is surrounded on every side by high land; the entrance being narrow and winding. Found here a Capt. Nimes of Groton Bank, Connecticut, with his ship, having brought around Cape Horn a load of Coal for the Steamers. I went ashore at about 9 1/2 O'clock & remained until 2 P.M. Acapulco contains about 5000 inhabitants. Houses are better, people are better clothed & look more intelligent than on the Isthmus.

At about 3 O'clock P.M. we again started for San Francisco & did not again stop until our arrival at this place. Our [First Cabin] hours for meals on the Pacific have been: Breakfast at 8 1/2; Lunch at 12 & Dinner at 4 1/2. I have had a cup of coffee & a few crackers brot to my room every morning at 6 1/2 O'clock, but it did not relish very well & before I arrived here, I had got so that none of the victuals tasted good to me. I have been taking solid comfort since I have come ashore.

Have seen quite a number of Whales, Sea Turtles &c. during the last few days of our voyage. After leaving the Isthmus, for several nights I spread my overcoat on the deck & slept in the open air with no covering on me except what I wore during the day. It was too hot to sleep in the close, little State room allotted me.[44]

The *Alta California*, on June 21, 1863, claimed passengers had a lark:

A Pleasant Voyage — Passengers who arrived on the steamer *Orizaba* speak in 'glowing' terms of the voyage from New York, which proved to be uninterruptedly pleasant so far as the weather was concerned; and the accommodations on the *Ocean Queen* were superior to those of the other vessels on the Atlantic side. The *Ocean Queen* was escorted among the West Indian Islands, and for 100 miles beyond, by a Federal war steamer.

In April 1864, the Reverend Henry W. Bellows, president of the United States Sanitary Commission, arrived in California on the *Constitution* to take the place of the deceased but already legendary Thomas Starr King and to collect money for sick and wounded soldiers.

Bellows, after sailing on a crowded, dirty, noisy Vanderbilt ship on the Atlantic, boarded the *Constitution* and exclaimed, "It was like going from the coal-hole to the parlor."

What do passengers do aboard ship? They eat, and the ships carried live beef, sheep, pigs, and poultry. "The cuisine is French — various, abundant and luxurious," Bellows recorded, and it reminded him of New York's "Fifth Avenue hotel, so far as freshness of provisions, variety and excellence of cookery, or nicety of service are concerned."

One day, Bellows joined the captain on his noon inspection trip and the kitchen had difficulty retaining its "A" rating. "The cook complains that the commodore rubs his white handkerchief upon his saucepans, and punishes him if any smut comes off," Bellows wrote. He added, "This inspection system is rigorously carried on twice every day."[45]

A year later, a gentleman known only as "Will" described his experiences to friends at Mokelumne Hill:

Steamer Golden City
October 30th 1865

Dear Friends All:

Tomorrow morning we expect to arrive at Panama. I shall be busy then getting my things ready, so will write you this evening. I wrote you last just before our arrival at Acapulco. We arrived at that place at 9 A.M. and remained there until 2 P.M. I with a great many others went ashore and rambled around the town for two or three hours. It is rather a forlorn looking place now, but the orange, lemon, and coconut groves, which surround it, are beautiful. The fort is dismantled, and in possession of the French. [On June 3, 1864, the French, with three frigates, landed 800 men and 65 cavalrymen, and captured the town for their puppet Emperor Maximilian I.]

Bought a few bananas there which were nice. The oranges were not ripe. The natives had some of the finest specimens of shellwork that I ever saw; would have bot one or two pieces if I had had any way to carry them home. We have been sailing along close in shore ever since we left Acapulco, and the scenery has been splendid.

I am getting along first rate. Four of us bought some ice tickets [at 7 cents a pound] and have ice water for dinner and supper. I can't drink their tea and coffee. We have plenty of sugar, but milk only a per cent of the time. I bribed my waiter shortly after we left San Francisco, so I get a great many accommodations and extras at the table. I have eaten that can of peaches, which were very fine. I relish the jelly and the blackberry wine — wish I had a gallon of the latter. I have not opened my trunk yet, and shan't until we get on the other side. Our baggage was weighed & checked on Saturday [28th]. My trunk only weighed 80 pounds [of 100 allowed]. Those apples are splendid; have one or two left of those I put in my valise.

There are over 1200 passengers on board; some say there are nearer 1400 — and among them are fully 100 children under 12 years of age. So you may know what a constant Bedlam we are in. We play cards a great deal. It is still raining & very cool. We shall have a nice little jam on the *Ocean Queen*. Don't you pity us?

Good Bye & love to all

WILL
[P.S.] There has been but very little sea sickness among the passengers. Have had a fine smooth sea all the way from S.F. Hope we may have it as smooth on the Atlantic.[46]

About 1870, society matron Mrs. Richard L. Ogden gave advice to her three daughters sailing west. If they had any money, "put it in a *little* cotton bag, & sew it to your Flannel shirt." Safety overrode comfort.

Once on board the Pacific Mail steamer, she opined,

You will be about 25 days coming. The Steamer on *this side* is in sight of land all the way up, except when she crosses the Gulf of California. After *two days out*, you are in a warm climate, and on the Isthmus in the Tropics, of course, and will require *Fans*, and lighter clothes, but do not take off your flannels, but *fan* yourselves cool, as you will have nothing else to do, as Mary used to say, 'Lay back and Fan.'

"Lay back and fan," a fitting closing for days on the Pacific Mail's Panama route.[47]

SS **CHINA** (I)– *The small but elegant salon of this William Webb-built ship (1866) has been beautifully refurbished with finely inlaid woods and leaded-glass windows, and stands over the water at Belvedere (Marin County) as a small museum. The* **China** *and three sisterships (***Japan, America, Great Republic***) were built specifically to inaugurate the China service but were not ready for the inaugural voyage (made instead by the SS* **Colorado** *on Jan. 1, 1867).* **China** *could carry 500 first and second cabin passengers and 800 in steerage, which is how many Nineteenth Century Chinese and Japanese immigrants found their way to America. Originally christened* **Celestial Empire**, *the* **China** *remained in PMSS trans-Pacific service until 1883 and was broken up in 1886. This original litho was made by Endicott of New York, ca. 1867. From the collection of Stephen J. and Jeremy W. Potash. Photo by Cathy Forbes.*

9

TO CHINA AND BEYOND

In 1866, the Pacific Mail built four huge wooden steamers, the *America*, *China*, *Great Republic*, and *Japan*, to fulfill their 1865 mail contract. With lengths of over 360 feet, the required strength and rigidity was provided by 4-foot-thick hulls and two sets of diagonal iron strapping. These were $1 million vessels. Naval historians John Haskell Kemble and Cedric Ridgely-Nevitt observe they were "the largest and finest wood steamships ever built anywhere." Yet, the rest of the world was switching to iron hulls and still-temperamental screw propeller propulsion.[48]

The 360-foot, 3,800-ton *China* was the last of William H. Webb's Pacific Mail steamers, for in 1866, he became president of the rival North American Steamship Company. Although the palatial *China* was the smallest of the steamers, one passenger exclaimed, "We enjoy an uninterrupted promenade seven hundred feet in circuit on the upper deck." Henry Steers then built the 360-foot, 3,900-ton *Great Republic* in 1867, which carried 250 first and 1,200 steerage passengers.[49]

In 1868, Steers finished the 362-foot, 4,350-ton *Japan*. The *Japan* could carry 122 first class passengers and 908 in steerage — plus 1,438 tons of coal and 2,100 tons by volume of cargo. Finally, in 1869, came the largest of the steamers, the 363-foot, 4,450-ton *America*. Aside from a dozen officers and other positions, beginning in 1867 about seventy-five Chinese crewed these wooden monsters to bring crew strength to 110. These great wooden ships were the last from the New York shipyards; modern iron ships were built elsewhere. [50]

P.M.S.S. CO'S 'CHINA'

The proud red-white-blue-white-red swallowtail Pacific Mail house flag flies over the 5,100-ton, iron-hulled screw propeller **China** *(II). Elegantly built in Scotland in 1889, she carried a crew of 150. Appropriately for her name, 120 of the crew were Chinese. She gave the Pacific Mail good service for a quarter-century. Image from the collection of Robert Chandler.*

*Shown around 1870, the slender 362-foot PMSS **Japan** rests in the Hunters Point drydock, with her port paddlewheel showing. Although these long wooden ships had extensive fire-fighting apparatus, the **Japan** burned at sea on December 17, 1874, between Hong Kong and Yokohama, with the loss of 415 passengers and crew. Spontaneous combustion in a coal bunker was the cause. Image from the collection of Robert Chandler.*

Huge, reliable, and repairable, 1800-horse-power walking beam engines drove the 40-foot wheels at 10 revolutions a minute steadily at 9.5 knots. Coal, as usual, was scarce and expensive at $11 a ton. The Pacific Mail had neither coaling stations nor repair facilities between San Francisco and Yokohama, 5,200 miles away. Bunkers held 1,500 tons of coal, of which the steamer used a reasonable forty-five tons per day for its 240 knots. Engine parts and spare masts were also aboard.

The ten-year agreement with the Federal Government called for twelve monthly round trips annually at a subsidy of $500,000. The ships sailed between 30 and 35 degrees north latitude and could have arrived in eighteen days. However, any captain arriving early and throwing off the printed schedule could be fired.

Trips averaged twenty-three days, twenty hours between San Francisco and Yokohama, and thirty-three days to or from Hong Kong, 7,300 miles direct from the Golden Gate. When the *China* sailed at noon on July 1, 1871, the ship's officers told Baron de Hübner, "On the 24th at 9 o'clock in the morning, you will land in Yokohama."[51]

Captain John Cavarly once wrote to his daughters, "It's a long, long way over this big ocean from S.F. to Yokohama." The highlight of any voyage became the mid-ocean meeting between the outbound and inbound mail steamers. For the two captains, it was a point of honor.[52]

On September 6, 1870, one passenger wrote, "At seven o'clock, precisely the hour which the captain had foretold, the ship *America*, eighteen days from Yokohama, appeared in a direct line before us, under full pressure, and with square sails set." The ships stopped abreast, exchanged mail and newspapers, and then "the walking-beams of the two giant ships gracefully bowed to each other, the wheels gently revolved, the passengers repeated their cheers, and a gun from either deck announced that the meeting was over."[53]

Outbound, the black-hulled ships carried 2,000 to 2,800 pounds of famed California flour and treasure — gold and silver bars and Mexican and U.S. Trade Dollars, the latter coined at the San Francisco Museum and Historical Society's new home in the U.S. Mint building at Fifth and Mission streets. The return trips brought back rice, tea, silk, and general Chinese goods.

Chinese passengers at $40 steerage brought good revenue, approximately $32,000 sailing to Hong Kong and $40,000 from immigrants coming to San Francisco. The large ventilated and clean berth deck could easily accommodate 1,000 Chinese, while their own galley served rice, dried fish, fresh pork, boiled cabbage, stewed daikon, and ducks eggs.

For the forty or so "Port Out, Starboard Home" [posh] first class travelers in the tropics, the comfortable upper decks, high above the spray, were opened to the winds and shaded. Their broad beams made the ships easy riders, while travelers praised the cleanliness, comfort, efficiency, elegance, and spaciousness.

A French nobleman wrote, "We lead a sort of country-house life, only the country house moves, and moves us with it." Being at sea board the *Colorado* in 1867, watching "the track traced each day in the blue waters," constantly amazed him. "Conversations with travelers from all parts of the world, the interest of the navigation, and the sight always the same and always new, of the magnificent sunsets — form the interests of each day."

Gold-accented peach blossom, lavender, and pea-green made for grand public areas, while deck planking alternated between black walnut and light-colored

Pacific Mail steamers, in addition to opening regular trans-Pacific steamship trade in commodities and luxury travel, also became the vehicle by which generations of Chinese, Japanese, and other Asian emigrants could make their way to America. Passage in a ship's steerage compartment was clearly lacking in comfort, as seen in this hand-colored lithograph of Chinese emigrants aboard Pacific Mail's SS **Alaska**, *from the May 20, 1876 issue of* **Harper's Weekly**. *From the collection of Stephen J. and Jeremy W. Potash. Photo by Cathy Forbes.*

spruce. Deck housings glistened white. The nobleman observed that this "vessel really shines like a mirror," which was no wonder: Captain George E. Lane made "a thorough inspection of the ship twice a day, goes into every cabin, into kitchens, and in fact everywhere."[54]

On the cooking side, the kitchen staff, chief steward, and his assistants were German. In the opinion of one traveler on the *China* in 1871, the two Germans in the dining room were merely "idlers." Regulated by bells, thirty-two Chinese waiters, dressed alike in black caps, queues to their heels, dark blue tunics, wide trousers, white socks, and black shoes, did all the work, quietly tending the twenty-two guests.[55]

One day in 1870, before the *China* reached Yokohama, a first cabin traveler penned, "Every inch of the deck, bulwarks, stanchions, rigging, and boats has been scoured, tarred, or painted." The 500 Chinese steerage passengers gathered on the foredeck, dressed in their best, and dropped "handfuls of rice and small pieces of colored paper into the sea, to propitiate the gods for a safe arrival."[56]

Passengers paid for their comforts. Fares were comparable to Panama in the 1850s and 1860s, and similarly governed by competition. In 1867, first class cost $250 to Yokohama and $300 to Hong Kong. Rivalry in 1874 with the Occidental & Oriental Steamship Company brought a reduction to $150 and $200, but with agreement in 1880, fares climbed back to $250. On January 10, 1881, the Pacific Mail took pleasure in announcing that "to stimulate and encourage travel to Japan, as a delightful resort for the purpose of health or of pleasure, it will hereafter issue Excursion Tickets from San Francisco to Yokohama and Return, at a rate of three hundred and fifty dollars for the Round Trip."[57]

The wooden palaces barely made it through the 1870s. The *America* was the first steamer to go, mysteriously burning at Yokohama in 1872 with a loss of fifty-nine; the *Japan* burned at sea in 1874, due to spontaneous combustion in a coal bunker, killing 415 souls; the *Great Republic's* bones have been at the mouth of the Columbia river since 1879. In that year, Webb's fine *China* made the

SS **GREAT REPUBLIC** – *One of the* **China**'s *sisterships, built specifically for the China trade, this vessel is depicted in an Endicott lithograph (ca. 1867) in Yokohama Harbor with Mt. Fuji in the distant background. She was built to carry 250 cabin and 1,200 steerage passengers, plus 2,000 tons of cargo and 1,500 tons of coal. These wooden side-wheelers were already outdated when they entered service, but they could churn their way across the Pacific with such reliability that east- and westbound paddlers could invariably meet and exchange mails at a predetermined mid-Pacific point and time. From the collection of Stephen J. and Jeremy W. Potash. Photo by Cathy Forbes.*

last trip by a wooden sidewheeler, her thirty-first, and in 1886, went to the wreckers. Yet a small, but elegant cabin, the only portion of a Webb-built ship surviving, stands refurbished on the waterfront at Belvedere, available for touring and parties.

The 1870s brought the Pacific Mail Steamship Company ownership turmoil. Too many controllers were only stock and railroad speculators, including rambunctious Jay Gould and slippery Trenor W. Park, a former associate of John C. Frémont. Quickly, the company suspended dividends. When the Pacific Mail did reinstate them in the 1880s, they returned at only 2 to 3 percent. Continual fights with other large transportation companies, including the once-friendly Panama Railroad, sapped the Pacific Mail's strength.

Still, without the benefit of current laws and accounting practices, the Pacific Mail had to remain profitable. Initiating the Far East venture cost $6 million in the late 1860s. For the first five round trips in 1867, only the government subsidy provided profit. Pacific Mail spent $670,000 to run the ships. On the revenue side, passengers and freight returned $610,000 and the U.S. Mails brought in $200,000, giving the company $140,000 in profit.

In the early 1870s, the company modernized its Asian fleet. Through various mail contracts and commercial ventures, the Pacific Mail served Japan, China, Australia, and the Central American coast to Panama. In 1873, the Pacific Mail fleet reached its maximum size at forty ships; three years later, thirty-three steamers called at forty-seven Pacific ports. By 1876, passengers and freight cleared $60,000 above expenses; the mail subsidy became gravy.

On January 28, 1874, the financial statement did not look good. For the quarter ending October 31, 1873, the Pacific Mail earned $1,305,000, but spent $1,342,000, to post a loss of $27,000. The president stated the obvious:

> It is also distinctively apparent that the old side-wheel wooden steamers have not been used with any profit to the Company, and that the substitution of the iron propeller has become an absolute prerequisite to future success.

A committee reaffirmed that truth when it looked back at land delivery of the mail during the 1860s. It said, "The fact exists that side-wheel wooden ships can no more successfully compete with the modern iron propeller in the carrying trade of the world than the stagecoach can compete with the locomotive." An afterthought followed: "It is a matter of regret that this fact was not earlier recognized."[58]

With this mandate, in 1874, John Roach & Sons of Chester, Pennsylvania, built the 5,100-ton iron screw steamers *City of Peking* and *City of Tokio*. At 423 feet long, with 48-foot beams, they were the largest ships flying the American flag.

With a crew of 120, about eighty-five would be Chinese. In 1878, the *City of Peking*, which could carry 1,650 passengers at 15 knots, reached San Francisco in twenty-six days from Hong Kong and in sixteen days, thirteen hours from Yokohama.

The *Alta*, on June 20, 1887, presented a typical arrival notice:

> **The China steamer** *City of Peking* **arrived at 2:50 P.M. yesterday, from Hong Kong, after a very fine passage. She brought sixteen European and 1,039 Chinese passengers, 2,406 tons of cargo, $33,900 in treasure, and forty packages of United States mail.**

She sailed until 1908.

In 1878, Roach turned out the luxurious 345-foot, 3,500-ton *City of Rio de Janeiro* for the Atlantic trade. She carried ninety first class passengers and 200 in steerage, and boasted a grand saloon 130 feet long and 30 feet wide. Pacific Mail bought her in 1881, and Captain John M. Cavarly brought her round the Horn. "I'm fighting her all the way," he wrote home. "It's as if she doesn't

MEETING OF THE STEAMERS IN MID-OCEAN.

On September 6, 1870, the smallest and the largest Pacific Mail paddlers met halfway. The 3,800-ton westbound **China,** *captained by John H. Freeman, greeted Captain Edward R. Warsaw's 4,450-ton eastbound* **America.** *Image from William H. Seward's* **Travels Around the World.**

want to come out to the Pacific."[59]

The *City of Rio de Janeiro* saw service to the Far East and transporting troops to the Philippines during the Spanish-American War. The steamer was entering San Francisco Bay through dense fog on Washington's Birthday 1901, when a crunching sound on the rocks near Fort Point meant death for 131 passengers and crew. Tall tales concerning a treasure in silver continue to swirl around the wreck like that deadly fog.

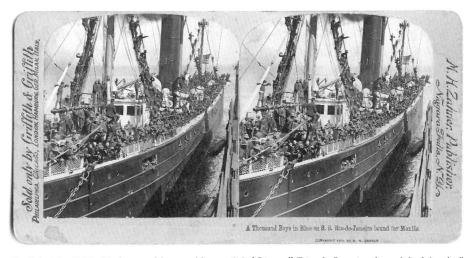

On July 22, 1898, "A thousand boys in blue on S.S. [City of] **Rio de Janeiro** *bound for Manila." During the Spanish-American War, the government charted Pacific Mail steamships as troop transports. On Washington's Birthday 1901, the* **City of Rio de Janeiro** *attempted to enter the Golden Gate in a heavy fog, struck the rocks near Fort Point, slid off, and sank in ten minutes with 128 souls. Stereo photograph from the collection of Robert Chandler.*

SS **CITY OF PEKING AT WAR** – *Lithograph at left, made in 1898 by Britton & Rey, San Francisco, depicts the ship as she departs San Francisco for the Spanish-American War in the Philippines. Her cargo: The First California Regiment US Volunteers.*
Other Pacific Mail vessels were also conscripted.
From the collection of Stephen J. and Jeremy W. Potash. Photo by Cathy Forbes.

CITY OF PEKING – *In the 1870s, Pacific Mail finally entered the age of iron, screw-propelled ships, which began to replace the romantic side-wheelers. This mighty passenger-freighter was painted in oils in the "Chinese School" ca. 1874 as she steamed into Hong Kong Harbour, probably on her maiden voyage from San Francisco. Chinese artists would paint the sky and the sea on various canvases, and wait for a ship's captain to commission the painting of the ship itself on a pre-painted background of his choice.* **City of Peking** *(sister ship was* **City of Tokio***) was to serve the company well for some 35 years. Years later, in 1989,*

after she had slowly become submerged in the mud near Candlestick Point, the **San Francisco Chronicle** *reported that a large piece of rusty iron had been found during excavations in that area. Officials of the San Francisco Maritime Museum identified the iron hulk as part of the hull of the* **City of Peking** *– in her day, the largest and fastest ship on the Pacific.*
From the collection of Stephen J. and Jeremy W. Potash. Photo by Richard Langs.

In 1889, the Fairfield Shipyard at Govan, Glasgow, known for its quality passenger liners, built the 5,100-ton *China* (II). A crew of 150, including 120 Chinese, ran the ship. Schedules called for the three *Cities* and the *China* to make Yokohama within seventeen days and Hong Kong within twenty-six.

In 1927, Englishman Will Lawson, a student of Pacific ocean steamers, remarked that "the Pacific Mail Company had a reputation for dropping out of services, after spending money, just before they became payable." Its fleet declined to twenty-three in 1880 and twenty in 1893, when the Southern Pacific Railroad took full control.[60]

In 1898, the Pacific Mail was determined to regain and maintain supremacy in Asian waters. It ordered two huge 11,300-ton steamers, the *Korea* and *Siberia*, which entered service in 1902. The 13,600-ton *Manchuria* and *Mongolia*, 615 feet in length, 65 in beam, followed in 1904 at 15 knots, carrying 260 passengers. No other shipping firm could match them for size. Crews reached 270, with about 225 Chinese.

"We are started sailing through the Golden Gate. Magnificent views," a passenger wrote on board the *Korea* on November 18, 1903. "I will send this postal [card] back by the Pilot's boat." On the same ship, ten years later, "It has been a bit rough," another passenger commented on November 18, 1914. "One wave yesterday coming clear up over the bridge and sloshing around all over."

SS **KOREA** – *Introduced in 1903, the twin-screw, 18-knot* **Korea** *and her sister ship, the* **Siberia**, *at 11,300 tons each, "easily outclassed in speed, comfort and capacity any competing ships," according to John Niven in his book* **The American President Lines and its Forebears**. *The SS* **China** *(II) joined them in the trans-Pacific. This bold image, published in 1903 by American Lithographic Company of New York and based on artwork by Fred Pansing, features on its frame the original brass name plate that directed inquirers to a PMSS sales office in Boston. From the collection of Stephen J. and Jeremy W. Potash. Photo by Richard Langs.*

Still, she found everything "very pleasant. We have all sorts of deck sports and dances every evening, and when we consider the seven meals and one nap a day, one can realize that the time passes quite rapidly." She then paused, "It is perfectly beautiful now and I want to go out and get some photographs of a family of Japs in the steerage, including two very charming children."

During this era, a passenger aboard the larger *Manchuria* experienced a little excitement entering Honolulu harbor. She began, "On a Coral Reef, August 20, 1906," continuing with the salutatory,

Dear Land People:
  'Tis half past nine. We were awakened this morning at five by the jangle and chatter of the Chinese. The boat lurched back and forth with now and then a sort of thud. I thought it no more nor less than rough weather. Looking out, it was entirely dark. Back I went to bed. The Oriental chatter still continued. Just the same, Mary said get

SS **MANCHURIA** – *With its brilliant blue hues and charmingly primitive style, this Chinese School painting (ca. 1904) depicts the San Francisco-based* **Manchuria**, *presumably on her maiden call at Hong Kong. She and her luxury-liner sister ship, the* **Mongolia**, *later became the* **President Johnson** *(I) and the* **President Fillmore** *(I), respectively, for Dollar Lines, and subsequently for American President Lines. From the collection of Stephen J. and Jeremy W. Potash. Photo by Cathy Forbes.*

CITY OF SYDNEY – *Important trading partners for San Francisco as early as the 1870s were Australia and New Zealand. This ship, built in 1875, and her sister ship, the* **City of New York,** *served that trade, and also supported a mail contract from Down Under. This is a China School painting of the ship made about 1875, probably in waters under British dominion. From the collection of Stephen J. and Jeremy W. Potash. Photo by Richard Langs.*

up and dress and see what it is. The boat had struck a coral reef and was rocking back and forth.[61]

The coast trade to Panama also proved profitable. In 1907, a committee from the San Francisco Chamber of Commerce reported that sailings every ten days, with calls at sixteen ports, pleased merchants exporting wine, brandy, canned and dried fruits, canned salmon, grain, beans, nuts, honey, wool, hides, asphalt, fuel oil, and redwood lumber. "Mercantile firms engaged in the Central American trade generally speak well of the past and present service of the Pacific Mail Steamship Company."[62]

Yet, commerce, like passenger liners, sometimes travels in unusual channels, and 1915 was one such year. The Panama Canal opened on August 15, 1914, bringing out fast east coast ships, a 1912 law prohibited railroad-owned steamships from using the canal, and Senator "Fighting Bob" La Follette's 1915 Seamen's Act to encourage hiring of American crews brought the discharge of lower-paid Chinese.

SS **STANLEY DOLLAR** – *In 1902, when this Chinese School painting was made of the freighter* **Stanley Dollar,** *the Dollar Steamship Company was building a potent freighting capability, initially for transportation of West Coast lumber. Dollar became a global trader, operating the "President" ships and introducing round-the-world services. Ultimately, in 1926, Pacific Mail would be folded into the Dollar Company. From the collection of Stephen J. and Jeremy W. Potash. Photo by Cathy Forbes.*

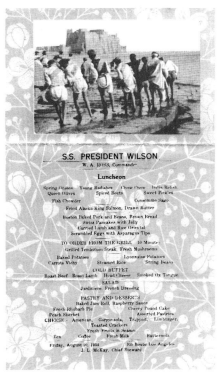

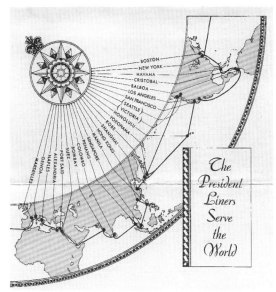

*A menu for lunch aboard Dollar Line's S.S. **President Wilson** on August 10, 1934, graphically displays how "The President Liners Serve the World" from Boston to Marseilles via Yokohama, Shanghai, and Bombay. From the collection of Robert Chandler.*

Europe, sodden in the gore of the bloody Great War, had abandoned the Pacific, while the war itself created a huge demand for shipping. Still, recalling Lawson's observation that the Pacific Mail would sell out just as its capital improvements became profitable, in August 1915, the Southern Pacific decided to sell its fleet of twelve ships. It sent the *China* and its four large twentieth-century ships to the Atlantic Transport Co. and the coasters to W.R. Grace & Co.

In 1917, with America's entry into World War I, the United States Shipping Board contracted existing ships and ordered new ones built. With ships available, Grace Line ownership built up the Pacific Mail fleet. Its three service areas were to Panama, calling at fourteen ports; on to New York via the canal; and sailings across the Pacific to Honolulu, the Philippines, Japan, and China.

Prominent after 1921 were five 535-foot, 14,100-ton, 18-knot Shipping Board steamers that carried 550 passengers. All, after 1922, bore presidential names: *Cleveland, Lincoln, Pierce, Taft,* and *Wilson.* Their time to Yokohama and Hong Kong remained the same as in the 1870s at

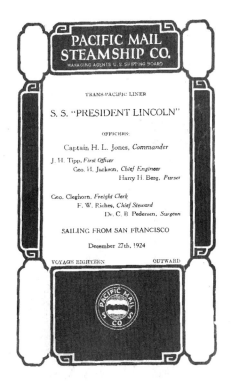

*Left: Title page for voyage No. 18 of SS **President Lincoln**, 1924. Right: back cover. Pacific Mail literature stressed that beautiful San Francisco was its home port. Robert Chandler collection.*

seventeen and twenty-six days. However, the ships also stopped at Honolulu and Shanghai. In 1921, the *President Wilson* set a record homeward bound of twelve days from Yokohama to Honolulu to San Francisco.

Although the Pacific Mail did well, fate determined otherwise. In 1925, the Shipping Board offered these five President liners for sale, and liked the bid terms and political connections of the Dollar Steamship Lines better. Exit Pacific Mail.

In 1921, Robert Dollar launched round-the-world service, and by registering trans-Pacific ships under the British flag, again hired Chinese crews. In 1937, the *President Coolidge*, launched in 1931, set a new record to Yokohama of nine days, nine hours, and fifty-one minutes. The next year, however, the Dollar Line went bankrupt. Under the 1936 Merchant Marine Act to subsidize U.S. flag ships, the Federal Maritime Commission seized its assets.

In 1938, the federal government began operating the ships as the American President Lines. Following World War II and the Korean War, the government sold the shipping line in 1952 to private investors headed by Ralph Davies. In 1954, Davies — San Francisco's Louise M. Davies Symphony Hall bears his wife's name — merged his shipping lines into Natomas Corporation, a gold-dredging business that went into oil production. Meantime, American President Lines found a new way to handle cargo.

The military, during World War II, developed and encouraged the idea of container shipping. On the east coast, trucker Malcolm P. McLean's appropriately-named shipping company Sea-Land created ship cargo containers that his trailer-trucks could haul or railroad cars could carry. Europe and the eastern United States quickly accepted container shipping. In the early 1960s, however, American President Lines had to convince Asian customers of the desirability of the new shipping technology and to build proper port cranes for loading and unloading. In 1967 and 1968, APL built six Pacesetter ships that could carry 1,200 20-foot containers.

A new base of operations came in 1973. Mechanization and modernization agreements

with the International Longshoremen's & Warehousemen's Union, beginning in 1961, banned loading cranes, and hence containers, in order to preserve jobs. Furthermore, piggy-backed container railcars could not clear the Portrero Hill tunnel. San Francisco promised new port facilities, but instead, "treated us shabbily," the president of American President Lines declared. The company moved to the Port of Oakland to take advantage of its investment in container cranes and direct railroad and freeway connections to the eastern United States. Corporate change came ten years later. A hostile takeover of Natomas spun off American President Lines in 1983. [63]

The next year, American President Lines found a better way to dispatch to interior ports ocean containers filled with high-value goods. It developed an innovative intermodal system with fast express trains rushing between major cities. Each train could carry 280 40-foot containers, one stacked on top of another. Of course, the company coordinated arrivals and departures of its trains (today operated by Pacer Stacktrain of Concord, California) with arrivals and departures of its ships.

In 1988, American President Lines operated twenty-three 21-man crew ships, 640 double-stack railcars holding ten 40-foot containers each, 35,000 truck chassis, and 77,000 containers to move goods from the ships direct to the recipients. The company's computer center controlled the cargo. American President Line's fleet, the largest in the Pacific, operated out of Oakland, Los Angeles, and Seattle to forty Asian ports. [64]

Singapore's Neptune Orient Lines acquired American President Lines (now known by its initials, "APL") in 1997 and built it into the sixth largest container line in the world. Today, the 67,000-ton *APL Spain*, launched in 2004 and not bearing a presidential name, is one of the company's largest cargo ships plying Pacific waters. She can carry 5,880 20-foot containers — or half that number of the more prevalent 40-foot containers. Since September 2004, the Singapore Government has owned sixty-eight percent of NOL, which in turn controls the 159-year-old shipping line that is still

SS **PRESIDENT HOOVER** – *When, in 1938, the Dollar Line folded and the name American President Lines took its place (today's APL), a San Francisco-based marketing department faced a grave dilemma: What to do with left-over Dollar Line promotional posters. Not only had the name (and logo) changed from Dollar Line (the dollar sign) to American President Lines (a stylized eagle), but the Dollar Line's poster-girl luxury liner, the SS **President Hoover**, had run aground off Taiwan and was judged a total loss. Clever marketers hand-painted red eagles over the Dollar signs on the image's two smoke stacks (the white curve of a Dollar sign can still be seen on the aft stack); painted out the name "President Hoover" on the bow (we have scratched off the paint to partially expose the name) so that one could assume the poster depicted her surviving sister, the **President Coolidge**; and removed the litho from its outdated Dollar Line frame to a hand-carved new frame bearing the name American President Lines. In this image lies the entire story of the 1938 transition. From the collection of Stephen J. and Jeremy W. Potash. Photo: Richard Langs.*

known by its symbol — a proud red eagle. APL has been highly profitable given the sharp increase in imports from China.

For more than a century and a half, Pacific Mail and its successors have set a record of service on the sea, including pioneering the Panama route, pioneering passenger service to the Far East, and in the modern era helping to revolutionize container shipping. However, the passage of time has storm-tossed its corporate entity. Prosperity, bankruptcy, and name changes have all intertwined, and what was once a proud American company is now foreign-owned. Still, 160 years since the founding of PMSS in 1848, the successor company helps to keep Pacific Mail's glorious history alive.

EPILOGUE

Word alone does not preserve the contributions that the Pacific Mail Steamship Company made to the development of California and the Pacific Basin. Historical structures significantly sustain the memory of the past. The vigorous city of Benicia, California, proud of its status as an early state capital and army arsenal, also glories that it was the site — as maritime historian and archeologist James P. Delgado states — of "the first major industrial enterprise of any sort on the Pacific Coast."

What company created this magnificent enterprise? It was the Pacific Mail Steamship Company. In 1850, it erected a coaling station, provisioning warehouse, and a repair facility at Benicia to service its ships at the northern end of the Panama-to-San Francisco route. Soon, an iron foundry was added to manufacture boilers, parts, and to repair the ships' engines.

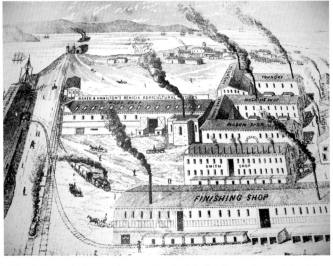

This lithograph depicts the vast Pacific Mail industrial complex of the 1850s in Benicia, California, after the property had been occupied in 1879 by a manufacturer of farm equipment. The coaling office is the small building with chimney in the center of the image, and the foundry is the large T-shaped building at the rear. Only these two buildings remain standing today. This photo courtesy of Benicia Historical Museum.

One can better envision the scope and importance of this complex with a look at the 1881 lithograph (detail) reproduced left. After Pacific Mail decided to concentrate its maintenance operations in San Francisco and left the property (1868-69), the facility was acquired in 1879 by the firm of Baker and Hamilton, who used it for their Benicia Agricultural Works, manufacturing plows and other farm implements, but retaining the original PMSS structures.

While a succession of firms, including Yuba Manufacturing (in 1914), used the stout structures for more than a century and a half, they fell into decay. In 2006, an arson fire gutted the foundry and coaling office, leaving only the shells. Still standing are only the coaling office (below, left) and the foundry building (below, right). Currently the Benicia Historical Society and other friends of the Pacific Mail Steamship Company are working to preserve them.

*Today, only the shells of the PMSS coaling office (left) and the iron foundry (right) are standing.
Photos courtesy of the Benicia Historical Museum; photographed by Cathy Forbes.*

End Notes

1. San Francisco *Alta California*, Aug. 28, 1854, Leonard to Sister Sarah, Jan. 19, 1857, Robert J. Chandler Collection.
2. Edwin L. Dunbaugh and William duBarry Thomas, William H. Webb Shipbuilder (Glen Cove, N.Y. Webb Institute of Naval Architecture, 1989), 173.
3. Thomas Rainey, *Ocean Steam Navigation and the Ocean Post* (New York: D. Appleton & Co., 1858), 183.
4. Edwin L. Dunbaugh and William duBarry Thomas, William H. Webb Shipbuilder (Glen Cove, N.Y. Webb Institute of Naval Architecture, 1989), 183.
5. Howland, photocopy courtesy of Mark T. Baker; *Alta*, Feb. 27, 1858.
6. *Alta*, May 6-8, 1858.
7. *Life, Diary and Letters of Oscar Lovell Shafter*, ed. by Flora Haines Apponyi Loughead (San Francisco: The Blair-Murdock Company, 1915), 158, 170.
8. San Francisco *Herald*, Feb. 14, 1855.
9. Albert D. Richardson, *Beyond the Mississippi* (Hartford, CT: American Publishing Company, 1867), 528.
10. Robert J. Chandler Collection.
11. John Haskell Kemble, *The Panama Route, 1848-1869* (Berkeley: University of California Press, 1943), tables 254-255.
12. John A. Stone, *Put's Original California Songster* (1856; San Francisco: D. E. Appleton & Co., 1868), 43-44.
13. Copy, Wells Fargo Bank Archives, San Francisco.
14. Circular, Robert J. Chandler Collection.
15. Mrs. Richard Ogden, San Francisco, Nov. 19, to Miss Kate F. Ogden, Bath, New York, Robert J. Chandler Collection.
16. Gilmore Meredith to PMSS Vice President Samuel W. Comstock, NY, photocopy courtesy of Joseph T. Silva.
17. Robert J. Chandler Collection.
18. Sarah, Robert J. Chandler Collection.
19. Robert J. Chandler Collection.
20. Robert J. Chandler Collection.
21. *Life, Diary and Letters of Oscar Lovell Shafter*, ed. by Flora Haines Apponyi Loughead (San Francisco: The Blair-Murdock Company, 1915), 70.
22. Robert J. Chandler Collection; *Alta*, May 1, 1855.
23. Dec. 21, 1851, July 19, 1852, to brother Henry Cutting, Boston; copy courtesy of Fred Holabird Americana.
24. Robert J. Chandler Collection.
25. c. 1947 notes by philatelist Edgar B. Jessup, Robert J. Chandler Collection.
26. Robert J. Chandler Collection.
27. Albert D. Richardson, *Beyond the Mississippi* (Hartford, CT: American Publishing Company, 1867), 527.
28. *Life, Diary and Letters of Oscar Lovell Shafter*, ed. by Flora Haines Apponyi Loughead (San Francisco: The Blair-Murdock Company, 1915), 200.
29. Cutting, Oct. 18, 1862; courtesy of Fred Holabird Americana.
30. Copy courtesy of Kenneth H. Harrison.
31. Covers or copies in Robert J. Chandler Collection; plus two letters; E.W. Horn, San Francisco, Feb. 1, 1865, to R.W. Horn, New York City.
32. Mrs. Charles V. Gillespie, San Francisco (corner of Kearny and Chestnut), Nov. 16, 1868, to her sister, Robert J. Chandler Collection; 1868 Contract – Overland Pacific Mails, HR Rep. #37, 40th Cong, 3rd sess. (1869), pp. 32, 153-7.
33. To mother Salinda Eastman, Robert J. Chandler Collection; *San Francisco Directory for the Year Commencing March 1877* (San Francisco: Henry G. Langley, 1877); "Chronological History of Current Events," p. 46.
34. James M. Parker's *San Francisco Directory for the Year 1852-53*, at page 102.
35. Copy, Wells Fargo Archives.
36. James A. Patterson, June 5, 1856, to General James W. Denver. Stanley Piller stock, transcribed on July 18, 2003; courtesy of Stanley Piller.
37. Joseph Howard, Jr., Sacramento, Mar. 4, May 17, 1859, to President John Freeman, Freeman & Co. letterpress copy book, Wells Fargo Archives.
38. Robert J. Chandler Collection.
39. Robert J. Chandler Collection.
40. John Haskell Kemble, *The Panama Route, 1848-1869* (Berkeley: University of California Press, 1943), 254, tally; 480,000 in, 296,000 out.
41. *Life, Diary and Letters of Oscar Lovell Shafter*, ed. by Flora Haines Apponyi Loughead (San Francisco: The Blair-Murdock Company, 1915), 37, 172; Elvineigh Kendrick, Stony Creek, July 19, 1857 to sister, Robert J. Chandler Collection.
42. Watsonville, Jan. 28, 1861, to D.J. Mosher, Clayville, New York, Robert J. Chandler Collection.
43. Robert J. Chandler Collection.
44. Robert J. Chandler Collection.
45. Henry W. Bellows, "Domestic Letters from the Pacific Coast," New York *Gazley's Pacific Monthly* 1 (April 1865): 299, 301.
46. Robert J. Chandler Collection.
47. Robert J. Chandler Collection.
48. Cedric Ridgely-Nevitt, *American Steamships on the Atlantic* (Newark: University of Delaware Press, 1981), 336.
49. Olive Risley Seward, ed., *William H. Seward's Travels Around the World* (New York: D. Appleton & Co., 1873), 31.
50. Robert J. Schwendinger, *Ocean of Bitter Dreams: Maritime Relations Between China and the United States, 1850-1915* (Tucson: Westernlore Press, 1988), 172-73, Chinese crews.
51. Joseph Alexander, Le Baron de Húbner, *A Ramble Around the World 1871- (1873)* Trans. by Elizabeth, Lady Herbert of Lea (London: Macmillan and Co., 1879), 183.
52. *City of Peking*, June 20, 1889, in Kathryn Hulme, *Annie's Captain* (Boston: Little, Brown and Company, 1961), 298.
53. Olive Risley Seward, ed., *William H. Seward's Travels Around the World* (New York: D. Appleton & Co., 1873), 32-33.
54. Ludovic, Marquis de Beauvoir, *The Conclusion of A Voyage Round the World by Marquis de Beauvoir: Pekin, Jeddo, and San Francisco* (1869 trans. Agnes and Helen Stephenson (London, John Murray, 1872), 236, 239, 243.
55. Joseph Alexander, Le Baron de Húbner, *A Ramble Around the World 1871- (1873)* Trans. by Elizabeth, Lady Herbert of Lea (London: Macmillan and Co., 1879), 193.
56. Olive Risley Seward, ed., *William H. Seward's Travels Around the World* (New York: D. Appleton & Co., 1873), 35.
57. Circular, Robert J. Chandler Collection.
58. *Alta*, Feb. 7, 1874.
59. Kathryn Hulme, *Annie's Captain* (Boston: Little, Brown and Company, 1961), 258.
60. Will Lawson, *Pacific Steamers* (Glasgow: Brown, Son & Ferguson, Ltd., 1927), 172.
61. M. E. Ritzman, Nov. 18, 1903; postcard, to E. A. Riegle, Gratz, PA; LaFayette L. Porter, to Mrs. M. M. Mathews, San Francisco; letter fragment to Mr. E. P. Clark, San Francisco, Robert J. Chandler Collection.
62. *Report of Harbor and Shipping committee of the Board of Trustees of the Chamber of Commerce of San Francisco upon Utility of Panama Route for Freight Transportation between San Francisco and the Atlantic States* (San Francisco: Neal Publishing Company, 1907), 10.
63. John Niven, *The American President Lines and Its Forebears, 1848-1984: From Paddlewheelers to Containerships* (Newark: University of Delaware Press, 1987) 251.
64. San Francisco *Chronicle*, Mar. 21, 1988.

BIBLIOGRAPHY

Much of this material is specialized. Niven provides the clearest and most concise summery of the Pacific Mail Steamship Company, while Coburn, Kemble, Wiltsee, and the Webb biography best integrate the interplay of the Gold Rush shipping companies. For day-to-day operations of everything Pacific Mail, see Kemble.

Beginnings and Pacific Mail Steamship Company Overview

Hubert Howe Bancroft, *California Inter Pocula* (San Francisco: The History Company, Publishers, 1888).

Robert J. Chandler, "Gold as a Cumbersome, Curmudgeonly Commodity, 1849-1970," *The Argonaut*, 13 (Winter 2002): 28-69.

Robert J. Chandler, "Steamer Days!" *Western Express* 52 (March 2002): 19-44, is an earlier variant of this PMSS study.

James P. Delgado, *To California By Sea: A Maritime History of the California Gold Rush* [to 1856] (Columbia: University of South Carolina Press, 1990). Besides experiences of the sea, Delgado details the growth of the port and the social, industrial, and governmental functions that came with it.

Memoirs of Robert Dollar, 4 vols. (W.S. Van Cott & Co., 1918 and 1921; privately printed, 1928).

Robert Dollar, *One Hundred and Thirty Years of Steam Navigation: A History of the Merchant Ship* (San Francisco: Robert Dollar Co., 1931).

Edwin L. Dunbaugh and William duBarry Thomas, *William H. Webb: Shipbuilder* (Glen Cove, N.Y. Webb Institute of Naval Architecture, 1989). In addition to insights on the masterful shipbuilder, it perceptively traces the history of the Pacific Mail and its competitors.

David I. Folkman, Jr., *The Nicaragua Route* (Salt Lake City: University of Utah Press, 1972).

John Haskell Kemble, "A Hundred Years of the Pacific Mail" *The American Neptune* 10 (1950), reprinted, Newport News, VA: The Mariners Museum, 1950. Kemble is the standard author on everything about the Pacific Mail. This article is good for the post Transcontinental Railroad history.

John Haskell Kemble, *The Panama Route, 1848-1869* (Berkeley: University of California Press, 1943; reprinted 1972, 1974; Columbia: University of South Carolina Press, 1990). The reprint also incorporates the material of earlier articles.

William Kooiman, *The Grace Ships, 1869-1969* (Point Reyes: Komar Publishing, 1990).

Will Larson, *Pacific Steamers* (Glasgow: Brown, Son & Ferguson, Ltd., 1927).

Oscar Lewis, *Sea Routes to the Gold Fields: The Migration by Water to California in 1849-1852* (New York: Alfred A. Knopf, 1949).

John Niven, *The American President Lines and Its Forebears, 1848-1984: From Paddlewheelers to Containerships* (Newark: University of Delaware Press, 1987).

Thomas Rainey, *Ocean Steam Navigation and the Ocean Post* (New York: D. Appleton & Co., 1858; reprinted 1977), gives the nuts and bolts of running a steamer, with emphasis on coal consumption. He has great praise for the Pacific Mail.

Report of Harbor and Shipping committee of the Board of Trustees of the Chamber of Commerce of San Francisco upon Utility of Panama Route for Freight Transportation between San Francisco and the Atlantic States (San Francisco: Neal Publishing Company, 1907).

Cedric Ridgely-Nevitt, *American Steamships on the Atlantic* [and Pacific] (Newark: University of Delaware Press, 1981). This professor at the Webb Institute knows his stuff!

Duncan S. Somerville, *The Aspinwall Empire* (Mystic, 1983).

Charles Beebe Stuart, *Naval and Mail Steamers of the United States* (New York: Charles B. Morton, 1853), is a fascinating illustrated book that includes the *Golden Gate* and its engines.

E. Mowbray Tate, *Transpacific Steam: The Story of Steam Navigation from the Pacific Coast of North America to the Far East and the Antipodes, 1867-1941* (New York: Cornwall Books, 1986).

Norman E. Tutorow, *The Governor: The Life and Legacy of Leland Stanford, A California Colossus*, 2 Vols (Spokane, WA: The Arthur H. Clark Company, 2004), discusses the competing Occidental & Oriental Steamship Company (1874-1908), II: 635-647.

U.S. Congress. Senate. *Report of Captain Thomas J. Cram on the Oceanic Routes to California*. 34th Cong., 3rd. sess., 1857. S. Doc. 51.

Victor Wolfgang Von Hagen, *Maya Explorer: John Lloyd Stephens and the Lost Cities of Central America and Yucután* (Norman: University of Oklahoma Press, 1947; reprint San Francisco: Chronicle Books, 1990). Stephens, memorialized by the steamer *John L. Stephens*, was archeologist, politician, and steamship proprietor.

Robert A. Weinstein, "North from Panama, West to the Orient: The Pacific Mail Steamship Company as photographed by Carleton E. Watkins," *California History* 57 (Spring 1978): 46-57.

Ernest A. Wiltsee, *Gold Rush Steamers* (San Francisco: The Grabhorn Press, 1938). The 1976 Quarterman Publications reprint contains 48 pages of additional steamer covers. Wiltsee's graceful style does not mask rightful and righteous indignation against fraud upon passengers and lives lost through incompetent seamanship.

China

Joseph Alexander, Le Baron de Húbner, *A Ramble Round the World 1871* (1873). Trans. by Elizabeth, Lady Herbert of Lea (London: Macmillan and Co., 1879). The Baron departed on July 1, 1871, on board the *China*.

Russell H. Conwell, *Why and How: Why the Chinese Emigrate, and the Means They Adopt for the Purpose of Reaching America* (Boston: Lee and Shepard, Publishers, 1871).

Richard C. Frajola, Michael O. Perlman, Lee C. Scamp, *The United States Post Offices in China and Japan, 1867 to 1874* (New York: The Collectors Club, 2006).

Kathryn Hulme, *Annie's Captain* (Boston: Little, Brown and Company, 1961) is the story of her grandmother, Annie Bolles, and grandfather, Pacific Mail Captain John Mansfield Cavarly. Cavarly commanded 22 ships during his 27 years with the Pacific Mail. At his retirement in 1894, he had captained 129 voyages to Panama in command of the paddlers *California*, *Constitution*, *Sacramento*, and *Sonora*, and the iron screw steamers *Colima* and *Granada*. Captain Cavarly took the iron *City of New York* to Australia, and made 13 voyages to Japan and China in charge of the wooden *China* and *Great Republic* and the iron *City of Peking* and *City of Rio de Janeiro*. He never lost a ship.

John Haskell Kemble, "Side-Wheelers Across the Pacific" *The American Neptune* 2 (1942) reprinted, San Francisco Museum of Science and Industry, 1942, is the best account on the Pacific Mail's wooden paddlers to China.

Ludovic, Marquis de Beauvoir, *The Conclusion of A Voyage Round the World by Marquis de Beauvoir: Pekin, Jeddo, and San Francisco* (1869). Trans. by Agnes and Helen Stephenson (London, John Murray, 1872). He sailed on the *Colorado*.

Edward D. G. Prime, *Around the World: Sketches of Travel through Many Lands and Over Many Seas* (New York: Harper & Brothers, 1872). The Reverend Prime left September 4, 1869, on the *Japan*. At sea, passengers published *The Ocean Wave*, a humorous newspaper, and held a mock trial of the purser for selling postage stamps at a premium.

Edward A. Rand, *All Aboard for Sunrise Lands: A Trip Through California and Across the Pacific to Japan, China and Australia* (Boston: D. Lothrop & Co., 1881, and reprinted). The Reverend Rand invites teenagers to join the Rogers boys, Ralph, 14, and Rick, 10, one spring Saturday aboard the *City of Tokio* bound for Asia.

Robert J. Schwendinger, *Ocean of Bitter Dreams: Maritime Relations between China and the United States, 1850-1915* (Tucson: Westernlore Press, 1988) details the employment of Chinese crews.

Olive Risley Seward, ed., *William H. Seward's Travels Around the World* (New York: D. Appleton & Co., 1873). Seward sailed on September 1, 1870, on board the *China*.

Mail Service

Stanley B. Ashbrook, "'Pan. & San. Fran. S.S.' [Mail Agent Steamer Markings, 1850-1852]," *The Stamp Specialist* (1944), contains correspondence of Atlantic steamer officer Joseph Chadwick 1850-1851.

Robert J. Chandler, "Vicissitudes of the Overland Mail in 1864," *Western Express* 51 (September 2001): 17-25.

Robert J. Chandler, "Wells Fargo's Stagecoaching: An 1860s Turf War," *Journal of the West* 42 (Spring 2003): 21-33; slightly revised, *California Territorial Quarterly* No. 69 (Spring 2007): 36-49, 51.

Jesse L. Coburn, *Letters of Gold: California Postal History through 1869* (Canton, OH: The U.S. Philatelic Classics Society, 1984) is the best available survey of express and mail service.

"The History of a Letter" in R.R. Olmsted, ed., *Scenes of Wonder and Curiosity from Hutchings' California Magazine, 1856-1861* (January 1858, II: 289-300; Berkeley: Howell-North, 1962).

Edgar B. Jessup, *et. al.*, *Early California Mail Bag*, 12 parts, Book Club of California Keepsake 1960 (San Francisco: 1960).

Henry C. Needham and Dr. Victor M. Berthold, "'Ahead of the Mails:' A Brief History of the Transportation of the U.S. Mail by Sea, 1848-1860," *The Collectors Club Philatelist* 7 (April 1928) illustrates early steamer covers.

Dr. Hugh P. Shellabear, "The Pacific Mail Steamship Company Straight Line Cancels on the 1862-72 Revenues," *American Revenuer*, December 1961, reprinted American Revenue Association.

Frank Soulé, John H. Gihon, and James Nisbet, *The Annals of San Francisco* (New York: D. Appleton & Company, 1855; reprinted Palo Alto: Louis Osborne, 1966; and Berkeley: Berkeley Hills Books, 1998), 626-638, contains a floridly-written account of "Steamer Day"—the departure of the *Brother Jonathan* and the arrival of the *Golden Gate*.

U.S. Congress. House. *Atlantic and Pacific Mails*. 36th Cong, 1st sess., 1860. H. Doc. 99. As a large number of first class letters went by land, President James Buchanan wished to raise the pay for the steamship companies that carried 15 tons of printed bulk material by sea.

____. *Mail Contracts with the Navy Department*. 31st Cong. 1st. sess. 1850. H. Doc. 52.

____. *Ocean Mail Steamers*. 33rd Cong, 2nd sess., 1854. H. Doc. 281, lists Arrivals and Departures from New York to Panama to San Francisco and Oregon, January 1852-March 1854.

Theron Wierenga, *The Gold Rush Mail Agents to California and their Postal Markings, 1849-1852* (Muskegon, MI: Theron Wierenga, 1987). Mail took one and one-third months to reach California until 1852, when the steamship companies reduced the time to a month.

Nicaragua Route Accounts

Mrs. James W. Likins, *Six Years Experience as a Book Agent* (San Francisco: Women's Print, 1874). On April 7, 1868, Amy Likins, 37, husband James, 43 and daughter Lucy 12, departed New York on the *Guiding Star* for Nicaragua. They arrived in San Francisco on May 8, on the *Moses Taylor*. This was the final voyage by that route.

Mark Twain, "Letter from 'Mark Twain'," San Francisco *Alta California*, January 18, February 22, 23, March 15, 16, 17, 23, 1867. Samuel Clemens sailed December 15, 1866 on the *America* via Nicaragua.

A.M.W. [Anna Maria Foster Wells], *Patty Williams's Voyage: A Story Almost Wholly True* (Boston: Walker, Wise, and Company, 1861). This is a children's book, reprinted in 1866 and 1869 about an 8-year old girl and her mother who come to California by way of Nicaragua to join her father.

Panama Railroad

Ira E. Bennett, *History of the Panama Canal: Its Construction and Builders* (Washington, D.C.: Historical Publishing Co., 1915).

Captain Julius Grigore, Jr., *Presidents of the Panama Railroad Company, 1849 to 1916*, with *A Brief Financial History of the Panama Railroad Company* (Print on demand, W.G. Guy, Publisher's Agent, Balboa, Republic of Panama, 2001)

Fessenden N. Otis, *Illustrated History of the Panama Railroad* (New York, Harper & Bros., 1861, and narrative portion only reprinted 1971). Otis published an expanded edition, 1867, while the article by "Oran" entitled "Panama Railroad," *Harper's New Monthly Magazine* 18 (January 1859): 145-169, is an early version.

Panama Route Memoirs

The arrival of the steamer *California* on February 28, 1849, the first trip on this route, has intrigued many: Victor M. Berthold, *The Pioneer Steamer California, 1848-1849* (Boston: Houghton Mifflin Company, 1932); Edward E. Dunbar, *The Romance of the Age; or, the Discovery of Gold in California* (New York: D. Appleton and Company, 1867); *The First Steamship Pioneers* and *Festival in Celebration of the Twenty-fifth Anniversary of the Arrival of the Steamer "California" . . . February 28, 1874*, (both San Francisco: H.S. Crocker & Co., 1874). This society of steamship pioneers formed in 1857. *Personal Memoranda: The Journal of his Voyage to California in 1848-1849*, by Samuel Hopkins Willey, the Founder of the University of California, edited by James M. Spitze (Berkeley: The Bancroft Library, 2007).

Henry W. Bellows, "Domestic Letters from the Pacific Coast, [April 9, 13, 20, 22, 1864]" New York, Gazley's *Pacific Monthly* 1 (April 1865): 294-301. He arrived April 30, 1864 on the *Constitution*.

Israel Joseph Benjamin, *Three Years in America, 1859-1862*. Trans. by Charles Reznikoff, 2 vols (Philadelphia: The Jewish Publication Society of America, 1956). Benjamin's voyage, from July 1 to July 24, 1860, was by *Ariel* and *Golden Age*, I: 109-115.

Margaret Kroh Blake-Alverson, *Sixty Years of California Song* ([Oakland] M.B. Alverson, 1913). This noted singer, her mother and four sisters arrived on the *Tennessee*, Captain George M. Totten, on December 14, 1851, fifteen days from Panama.

Samuel Bowles, *Across the Continent* (Springfield, MA: Samuel Bowles & Company, 1865). Bowles sailed on the *Golden City* on September 2, 1865.

Olive Colegrove [Mrs. Cornelius] Cole, "To California via Panama in 1852," *Annual Publications of the Historical Society of Southern California*, Vol. 9, part 3 (1914): 163-172.

James Miller Guinn, "To California via Panama in the Early '60s," *Annual Publication of the Historical Society of Southern California* 5 (1900): 13-21. Discharged Union veteran Guinn arrived on the Opposition Line's "Rolling *Moses*" *Taylor* on February 10, 1864, 17 days from Panama and 40 from New York.

William Ingraham Kip, *The Early Days of My Episcopate* (New York: Thomas Whittaker, 1892; reprinted, Oakland, Biobooks, 1954). Kip arrived January 29, 1854, on the *Golden Gate* and *Columbia*. See also Helen Rocca Goss, "An Ill-Starred Voyage: The S.S. *Golden Gate*, January 1854," *California Historical Society Quarterly* 32 (December 1963): 349-361.

Albert D. Richardson, *Beyond the Mississippi* (Hartford, CT: American Publishing Company, 1867). This New York *Tribune* reporter with great powers of observation left San Francisco on December 19, 1865, on the *Sacramento*.

Life, Dairy and Letters of Oscar Lovell Shafter, ed. by Flora Haines Apponyi Loughead (San Francisco: The Blair-Murdock Company, 1915). Shafter arrived on the *Golden Gate* on November 13, 1854, after 23 days, 15 hours from New York City.

Bayard Taylor, *Eldorado: or, Adventures in the Path of Empire* (New York: George P. Putnam, 1850; often reprinted). Taylor arrived August 18, 1849 on the *Oregon*.

William S. Walker, *Between the Tides* (Los Gatos: W.S. and Glenn Walker, Printers, 1885). Civil War veteran Walker arrived on the opposition *Moses Taylor* via Panama on May 25, 1864.

Shipwrecks

[*Brother Jonathan*] sailed on the Nicaragua route before becoming a coastal steamer and tragically sinking on July 30, 1865. An exhibit containing documents and recovered coins is on display at the Wells Fargo History Museum 420 Montgomery Street. Q. David Bowers, *The Treasure Ship S.S.* Brother Jonathan: *Her Life and Loss, 1850-1865* (Wolfeboro, NH: Bowers and Merena Galleries, Inc., 1999); Bowers and Merena Auction, Los Angeles, May 29, 1999, "The S.S. *Brother Jonathan* Treasure Coins;" Alfred L. Lomax, "*Brother Jonathan*: Pioneer Steamship on the Pacific Coast," *Oregon Historical Quarterly*, September 1959 and reprinted; and Dennis Powers, *Treasure Ship: the Legend and Legacy of the S.S.* Brother Jonathan (New York: Citadel Press, 2006).

[*Central America*] The fabulous treasure sent from San Francisco aboard the PMSS *Sonora* and was recovered from the connecting steamer *Central America* (formerly the *George Law*), which sank on September 12, 1857. Intriguingly, Frank Marryat, *Mountains and Molehills* (New York: Harper & Brothers, Publishers, 1855) praised this ship in 1854 for having life jackets at each bed (350-357). James P. Delgado, "'Their Bones Should be Left in the Ocean to Rot:' Notes on an Unusual Shipwreck Song," *Book Club of California Quarterly News-Letter* 49 (Spring 1984): 31-43, expresses contemporary shock at the tragedy and heavy loss of life. Further elaboration is in Q. David Bowers, *A California Gold Rush History Featuring the Treasure from the S.S.* Central America (Newport Beach: California Gold Marketing Group, 2002), a hefty 1,000 pages; *A Catalogue of Treasure from the S.S.* Central America (Newport Beach, CA: Monaco Financial, LLC. 2005); Christie's Sale No. 9562, "Gold Rush Treasures from the SS *Central America*," New York, December 14, 2000; Judy Conrad, ed. *Story of an American Tragedy: Survivors' Accounts of the Sinking of the Steamship* Central America (Columbus, OH: Columbus-American Discovery Group, Inc., 1988); Gary Kinder, *Ship of Gold in the Deep Blue Sea* (New York: The Atlantic Monthly Press, 1998); Normand E. Klare, *The Final Voyage of the* Central America, 1857 (Spokane, WA, The Arthur H. Clark Company, 1992); Sotheby's Sale NY 7415, "Treasures from the S.S. *Central America*," New York, December 8-9, 1999 [actually held June 20-21, 2000]; and wreck discoverer Tommy Thompson's *America's Lost Treasure* (New York: The Atlantic Monthly Press, 1998).

[*Golden Gate*] Andre Chavanne, "The Burning of the *Golden Gate* in July [27] 1862," trans and ed. by Desire Fricot, *Quarterly of the California Historical Society* 19 (March 1940).

[*Tennessee*] James P. Delgado and Stephen A. Haller, *Shipwrecks at the Golden Gate: A History of Vessel Losses from Duxbury Reef to Mussel Rock* (Nevada City, CA: Lexikos, 1989), has a section on the *Tennessee* wrecked on March 6, 1853; and Fred W. Stocking, "How We Gave a Name to Tennessee Cove" *Overland Monthly* 17 (April 1893).

U.S. Congress. House. [PMSS] *San Francisco Rescue*. 33rd Cong, 1st sess., 1854. H. Rept.113.

[*Winfield Scott*] *Memoirs of Edward Bosqui* (1904; Oakland: The Holmes Book Company, 1952). On board *Winfield Scott* wrecked on December 2, 1853, on Anacapa Island; James P. Delgado, "Watersoaked and Covered with Barnacles: The Wreck of the S.S. *Winfield Scott*," *Pacific Historian* 27 (Summer 1983): 1-21.

[*Yankee Blade*] Donald G. Knight and Eugene D. Wheeler, *Agony and Death on a Gold Rush Steamer: The Disastrous Sinking of the Side-Wheeler* Yankee Blade [*on October 1, 1853*] (Ventura: Pathfinder Publishing of California, 1990).

ABOUT THE AUTHORS

Co-authors Robert J. Chandler (left) and Stephen J. Potash with the Coke Wood Award from Westerners International for the best historical article or monograph of the year. The authors have expanded their 2005 monograph on the history of the Pacific Mail Steamship Company into the current book – Gold, Silk, Pioneers & Mail.

Bob Chandler received his doctorate in history in 1978 from the University of California, Riverside, for a dissertation on "The Press and Civil Liberties in California during the Civil War, 1861 to 1865." Since then, he has been the senior researcher for Historical Services, Wells Fargo Bank, and has written some fifty articles on Wells Fargo and Civil War California history. Two of his articles have appeared in *The Argonaut*. The author declares that his alter-ego is His Majesty, Norton I, Emperor of the United States and Protector of Mexico. He is chairman of the Emperor Norton Bridge Committee to properly name the Trans-Bay Bridge after its originator. Email: chandlersbasset@yahoo.com.

Steve Potash, a Pacific Mail collector and enthusiast for twenty-five years, is a Bay Area-based public relations consultant to the international trade and freight transportation sectors. He is an International Relations graduate of Pomona College, Claremont CA. Steve helped plan the first retrospective exhibition of the paintings of San Francisco's premier 19th Century maritime artist, William A. Coulter, held in 2006 at the San Francisco Maritime National Historical Park. After Bob Chandler succeeds in renaming the Bay Bridge for Emperor Norton I, Steve would like to sail under it aboard a perfect replica of Pacific Mail's first wooden side-wheeler, the SS *California* (1848). Email: steve@PotashCo.com.

INDEX

A

Adams & Co. 17, 24
Alabama 27
America 4, 6, 12, 33, 34, 35
American Express Company 24
American President Lines xi, 42
APL Spain 42
Ariel 27
Aspinwall 3, 5
Aspinwall, William Henry 1, 14, 15
Atlantic Transport Co. 41

B

Baker and Hamilton 44
Bancroft Library x
Bell, Gerritt W. 27
Bellows, Henry W. 31
Belvedere, California x,
Benicia, California x, 44
Benicia Agricultural Works 44
Benicia Historical Museum 44
Benicia Historical Society 44
Blethen, Capt. James H. 25
Book Club of California, The x
Broadway wharf 5
Brown, William H. 5
Brown Bros. 14

C

California 3, 15
Candlestick Cove x
Carolina 15
Carquinez Strait x
Cavarly, Capt. John M. 34, 37
Central America Transit Company
    12
Chamberlain, William E. 29
Charter Oak Life Insurance Com-
    pany 30
China (I) x, 33, 34, 35
    illustration 32
China (II) 38
    illustration 33
China Trade ix, xi

City of Peking x, 37
    illustration 38
City of Sydney
    illustration 40
City of Tokio 37
Colón 1. *See* Aspinwall
Colorado 7, 9, 26, 35
Columbus 15
Commercial Street 5
Constitution 7, 9, 27, 31
    illustration 16
Corbett, Henry W. 27
Crocker, Charles 26
Cunningham, Jr., William E. 8
Cutting, Ephraim 21

D

Davies, Ralph 42
Delgado, James P. 44
Dimon, John 4
Dollar, Robert 42
Dollar Line xi
Dollar Steamship Lines 42

E

Eastman, George L. 23
Ernest A. Wiltsee Collection 19

F

Fairfield Shipyard 38
Fargo, William G. 24
Federal Government
    mail subsidy 34
Federal Maritime Commission 42
Field, Stephen J. 27
Fitch, Russel 6
Flemming & Douglass 16
Folsom Street Wharf 5
Freeman & Co.'s Express 26
Freeman, John 26
Frémont, John C. 36

G

George Law's Line of Pacific Steam-
    ers 15

Golden Age 3, 5, 7, 19, 25
Golden City 7, 12, 23, 27
Golden Gate 3, 4, 5, 8, 9, 10, 17,
    19, 29
    illustration 4
Gold Rush x, 3, 15
gold standard
    in California 12
Gould, Jay 36
Great Republic x, 33, 35
    illustration 36
Great War 41

H

Harper's Monthly 23
Howland, William H. 4
Huntington, Colis 2
Huntington Library x
Hutchings, James M. 19

I

Independent Opposition Line 10
Indian war
    effects on mail delivery 22
International Longshoremen's &
    Warehousemen's Union 42

J

J.L. Stephens 6
J.M. Chapman 27
Jacob A. Westervelt & Co. 5
Japan 4, 33, 35
    photo 34
John L. Stephens 3, 4, 7, 17, 19, 20
    illustration 13
John Roach & Sons 37

K

Kelly, Michael 13
Kemble, John Haskell x, 33
Kimball, Charles P. 18
King, Thomas Starr 31
Knight, Samuel 27
Korea 38
    illustration 39

L

La Follette, Sen. Robert 40
Lane, Capt. George E. 35
Latimer, Benjamin G. 16
Law, George 16
Lawson, Will 38
Libby, Emma 20
Long Wharf 5
Louise M. Davies Symphony Hall 42
Lucy, S.S. 17

M

mail
  pre-paid and collect 18
Manchuria 38
  illustration 39
Martin, Prescott 18
McLane, Louis 26
McLean, Malcolm P. 42
Merchant Marine Act of 1936 42
Mongolia 38
Moses Taylor 4
Mosher, William C. 29

N

Natomas Corporation 42
Neptune Orient Lines 42
North American Steamship Company 12, 33
  successor to Central American Transit Company 14
Northern Light 25
North Star 29

O

Ocean Queen 14, 30
Ogden. Mrs. Richard L. 32
Oregon 3
Overland Mail 20, 21
Overland mail route 21

P

Pacer Stacktrain 42
Pacific Mail Steamship Company 44
  demise of 42
  expansion across the Pacific 33–35
  expenses and revenues 8–9
  incorporation of 1
  industrial plant construction in Benicia 5–6
  in the early 1900s 40–42
  Nicaragua route 10
  trans-Pacific fares 35–36

Pacific Street wharf 5
Palmer, Noyes S. 30
Panama x, 3, 16
Panama Canal 40
Panama Railroad Company 5
Park, Trenor W. 36
Parker, Samuel H. 21
Polk, James K. 3
President Cleveland 41
President Coolidge 42
President Hoover
  illustration 43
President Lincoln 41
President Pierce 41
President Taft 41
President Wilson 41

R

Rainey, Thomas 3
rates, steamship
  comparison 11
Richardson, Albert D. 20
Ridgely-Nevitt, Cedric 33
Rio de Janeiro 37
  photo 37
Robinson, Alfred 15

S

Sacramento 7, 9
San Francisco
  illustration 9
San Francisco ix
San Francisco Chamber of Commerce 40
San Francisco Chronicle 38
San Francisco Post Office operations 19
Seamen's Act of 1915 40
Shafter, Oscar L. 6, 21, 29
Siberia 38
Sierra Nevada 25
Singapore xi, 42
Smith, Stephen 4
Sonora 3, 5, 9, 18, 19
Southern Pacific 41
St. Louis 5
stagecoach
  use for mail 21
Stanley Dollar
  illustration 40
Steamer Day 1
steamer travel
  mid-1800s 29–31
Stephen Smith and John Dimon shipyard 3

Stone, John A. 10
Stout, Capt. W.C. 26
Sullivan, John W. "Jerry" 18

T

Tennessee x, 16
  illustration 2
transcontinental railroad
  effects on mail delivery 23
Twain, Mark 6

U

Uncle Sam 6, 10
  illustration 7
United States mail
  role in developing steamship companies 15
United States Mail Line 1
United States Mail Steamship Company 10
United States Sanitary Commission 31
United States Shipping Board 41

V

Vallejo Street Wharf 5
Vanderbilt, Cornelius 1, 10, 20

W

W.R. Grace & Co. 41
Ware, Jr., L. 27
Watkins, Commodore James T. 27
Webb, William H. 3, 4, 6, 14, 33
Webb Institute of Naval Architecture 3
Wells, Fargo & Co. 17
Wells, Fargo & Co.'s Express 24
Wells, Henry 24
Wells Fargo History Museum 19, 27
Wiltsee, Ernest x
Winfield Scott x
Winter, G. 16
Witner, Joseph 19

Y

Yankee Blade 10
Yuba Manufacturing 44

This printing is limited to five-hundred copies.